THE WAY OF THE
DESERT

Published by
The Bible Reading Fellowship
15 The Chambers, Vineyard
Abingdon OX14 3FE
United Kingdom
Tel: +44 (0)1865 319700
Email: enquiries@brf.org.uk
Website: www.brf.org.uk
BRF is a Registered Charity

ISBN 978 1 84101 798 3

First published 2011
10 9 8 7 6 5 4 3 2 1 0

Acknowledgments
Unless otherwise stated, scripture quotations are taken from the Holy Bible, Today's New
International Version, copyright © 2004 by International Bible Society, and are used by
permission of Hodder & Stoughton Publishers, a member of the Hachette Livre Group UK.
All rights reserved. 'TNIV' is a registered trademark of International Bible Society.

Scripture quotations taken from the Holy Bible, New International Version, copyright © 1973,
1978, 1984, 1995 by International Bible Society. Used by permission of Hodder & Stoughton
Publishers, a member of the Hachette Livre Group UK. All rights reserved. 'NIV' is a registered
trademark of International Bible Society. UK trademark number 1448790.

Extracts from the Authorised Version of the Bible (The King James Bible), the rights in which
are vested in the Crown, are reproduced by permission of the Crown's Patentee, Cambridge
University Press.

Scripture quotations from The Revised Standard Version of the Bible, copyright © 1946, 1952,
1971 by the Division of Christian Education of the National Council of the Churches of Christ
in the United States of America, are used by permission. All rights reserved.

Scripture quotations from The New Revised Standard Version of the Bible, Anglicised Edition,
copyright © 1989, 1995 by the Division of Christian Education of the National Council of the
Churches of Christ in the United States of America, are used by permission. All rights reserved.

A catalogue record for this book is available from the British Library

Printed in Singapore by Craft Print International Ltd

The paper used in the production of this publication was supplied by mills that source their
raw materials from sustainably managed forests. Soy-based inks were used in its printing and
the laminate film is biodegradable.

THE WAY OF THE
DESERT

Daily Bible readings through Lent to Easter

Andrew Watson

Acknowledgments

I am grateful to Pete Wilcox, David Urquhart and my wife Beverly for reading the first draft of this book and providing some most helpful comments; also to Naomi Starkey for her expert editorship of this and my previous books.

It was my grandmother, Dr Mary Watson, who first introduced me to the discipline of regular Bible reading when I was just seven years old; and I remain deeply thankful for her encouragement, and that of many others since who have inspired me—in the words of the Coronation service—to regard the Scriptures as 'the most valuable thing that this world affords'.

Andrew Watson has recorded a series of seven podcasts and YouTube clips on the contents of this book, which might prove helpful to individuals or in a small group setting. The first is an introduction to the book as a whole; the others introduce the themes of each of the six weeks of Lent and Holy Week.

To access this material, please visit www.brfonline.org.uk/the-way-of-the-desert/

CONTENTS

Week Four: Lessons from the desert

Week Five: Beyond the desert

Holy Week: The cross in the desert

Introduction

WHAT DID JESUS DO?

It became the must-have accessory among Christian young people in the 1990s: a rubber wristband cryptically inscribed with the letters WWJD. A hundred years earlier, Charles Sheldon, American pastor and Christian Socialist, had written a book entitled *What Would Jesus Do?* and the initials on the wristbands picked up just the same question. Whatever situations we face in life—whatever decisions we are called upon to make—the issue of WWJD is vital for the Christian disciple. Jesus' call, after all, is to 'follow me'.

As a church leader at the time when WWJD wristbands were selling by the truckload, I was therefore positive about this simple summons to Christian thinking and discipleship. My only reservation was that WWJD seemed to beg a prior question, and one on which our young people appeared increasingly hazy, namely 'What Did Jesus Do?' Short of marketing my own range of WDJD wristbands there were limited means to get my message across, though I mentioned it in the occasional sermon at the time. But the danger of asking speculative questions about Jesus without rooting them clearly in the Jesus of the Gospels is a real one. How easy to construct a Jesus of my own making, a pocket Jesus (or idol, to use the Bible's own term), who conveniently seems to share my views on politics, religion, money and relationships, without making me feel uncomfortable or challenged at all!

As we approach Lent, the question 'What did Jesus do?' yields some interesting answers: for the 40 days of Lent reflect the period that Jesus spent in the wilderness following his baptism and before the start of his public ministry. It's a period briefly mentioned by the Gospel writer Mark (1:12–13) and described in greater detail by fellow evangelists Matthew (4:1–11) and Luke (4:1–13). So what did Jesus do in what we could call the first Lent? According to Matthew and Luke, he fasted, he resisted a series of temptations and he meditated on some chapters from the book of Deuteronomy.

It's this last part that may not be too obvious to readers of the Gospels, unless we take the trouble to look up the three Bible verses with which Jesus responded to his spiritual opponent. In reply to each of the devil's temptations, Jesus used the formula 'It is written', then followed it with a verse from Deuteronomy 6 and 8. In my limited attempts to memorise Bible verses, it tends to be the parts I have just been learning that come to mind as I face the choices, pressures and temptations of the day. It doesn't take too big an imaginative leap to conclude that Jesus was meditating on the book of Deuteronomy (and perhaps, more broadly, on the whole story of the exodus) during his 40 days of fasting and prayer.

It's an assumption supported by Matthew, whose Gospel regularly seeks to parallel Jesus' life with the lives of the people of Israel during the days of the exodus. Referring to Joseph the carpenter's decision to make a detour to Egypt for a while, Matthew quotes some words from the prophet Hosea, 'Out of Egypt I called my son' (Matthew 2:15; Hosea 11:1). Leading us next to the River Jordan and to the sight of a crowd of Jews going down into the water to be baptised, another picture comes to mind of Israelite crowds 'going down into the water' at the miraculous parting of the Red Sea. As Jesus himself is then baptised and tested for 40 days and 40 nights, he is clearly aware of the 40 years in the wilderness which followed that mighty miracle; and when he next chooses to quote some of the key scriptures from those wilderness years, it is all of a piece with the story that Matthew is seeking to tell.

Jesus is thus the new Israel, the new example of what it means to be chosen and loved and holy. Yet while the Israel of the exodus frequently got it wrong—so providing a series of cautionary tales for us to learn from—the new Israel, Jesus himself, constantly gets it right, so offering a perfect model for us to follow.

As we turn with Jesus to the story of Israel's wilderness wanderings—a story that begins in Exodus 15 and ends with the close of the book of Deuteronomy—we have to admit that there is much here that is difficult, strange and hard to understand. There are long lists of names and numbers, detailed descriptions of sacrificial offerings and a prevalence of references to 'smiting' (for readers of the King James Version) or 'destroying' (for those who prefer something more contemporary). There are times when the last thing we would want to be is one of Israel's enemies, and other times when we quite understand Tevye's words in *Fiddler on the Roof*: 'We are your chosen people. But, once in a while, can't you choose someone else?'

To complicate matters further, there are different styles and preoccupations in these books (and even within individual passages), which have led Bible scholars to come up with some strongly argued theories as to when and how they were written. Reading contemporary Middle Eastern politics in the light of God's command to drive out the nations from the promised land is hardly a comfortable experience, either.

All in all, it's hardly surprising that a million Christian readers have made it their resolution to read the Bible from beginning to end, and have started well, with the colourful stories of Adam and Eve, Noah, Abraham, Jacob, Joseph and Moses' early years—only to find themselves bogged down by the middle of Leviticus and quietly deciding to spend more time with their family (or their TV) instead.

The question 'What did Jesus Do?', though, together with our suggestion that Jesus spent the first Lent meditating on Israel's time in the wilderness, implies that this part of the Bible, for all its difficulties, contains plenty to sustain us for 40 days and more. There's even a sense that every Christian story, each personal 'Pilgrim's Progress', mirrors the story of those desert years. We start with the parting of the Red Sea, with baptism and the beginnings of a freedom from the slavery of sin. We finish with the parting of the River Jordan, with death, resurrection and an entry into our spiritual inheritance; and meanwhile we experience life in the wilderness as a 'chosen people' on the one hand and 'aliens and strangers in the world' on the other (1 Peter 2:9, 11, NIV).

Our years on earth, in this understanding, become a training ground—an Olympic village where we engage in vigorous faith-building and learn to exercise our discipleship muscles to the full. At times our coach seems alarmingly strict. At times we may find ourselves making Tevye's question our own: 'Can't you choose someone else?' But as we look to Jesus, the 'author and perfecter of our faith, who for the joy set before him endured the cross, scorning its shame' (Hebrews 12:2, NIV), we know that this training is gloriously worthwhile, whatever the struggles and challenges along the way.

As we travel through Lent, Holy Week and Easter, then, we will begin our readings with Israel's entry into the desert, close them with Israel's entry into the promised land, and focus our main attention on the 40 years in the middle, on life in between. This desert, God's training ground, won't prove a comfortable spot in which to settle. Both the place itself and the scriptures that describe it will share at times a sense of wildness, unpredictability and danger. But just as Jesus' own life and ministry were tested and formed in that environment, so the same can be true for us. Indeed, we believe in a God who can make the 'wilderness blossom' and can reveal to us 'treasures of darkness, riches stored in secret places' (Isaiah 35:1; 45:3).

Our concern in the weeks to come will not be to unravel the often complex questions of exactly how these texts came into their final shape or to draw out the various sources and historical traditions that may lie behind them. Instead we will be taking the scriptures as they stand, much as Jesus himself did, seeking to apply them in the conviction that even some of the most challenging parts of the Bible are God's inspired word for us today.

And what better place to start than with a glorious hymn so beloved of the bass section of every church choir from the Welsh valleys to the ends of the earth? As the evening of Shrove Tuesday draws to a close—as the last pancake is eaten, the empty lemon skins are dropped in the compost bin, the frying pan is put away, the busy world is hushed and our work is done—let's use this hymn as a prayer for Lent and a prayer for life:

Guide me, O thou great Jehovah,
pilgrim though this barren land;
I am weak, but thou art mighty;
hold me with thy powerful hand;
Bread of heaven, Bread of heaven,
feed me now and evermore,
feed me now and evermore.

Open now the crystal fountain,
whence the healing stream doth flow;
let the fiery, cloudy pillar
lead me all my journey through;
strong Deliverer, strong Deliverer.
be thou still my Strength and Shield,
be thou still my Strength and Shield.

When I tread the verge of Jordan,
bid my anxious fears subside;
Death of death, and hell's destruction,
land me safe on Canaan's side;
songs of praises, songs of praises,
I will ever give to thee,
I will ever give to thee.
WILLIAM WILLIAMS (1745)

1

ASH WEDNESDAY: CREATION

As Pharaoh approached, the Israelites looked up, and there were the Egyptians, marching after them. They were terrified and cried out to the Lord. They said to Moses, 'Was it because there were no graves in Egypt that you brought us to the desert to die? What have you done to us by bringing us out of Egypt? Didn't we say to you in Egypt, "Leave us alone; let us serve the Egyptians"? It would have been better for us to serve the Egyptians than to die in the desert!' Moses answered the people, 'Do not be afraid. Stand firm and you will see the deliverance the Lord will bring you today. The Egyptians you see today you will never see again. The Lord will fight for you; you need only to be still.' … Then Moses stretched out his hand over the sea, and all that night the Lord drove the sea back with a strong east wind and turned it into dry land. The waters were divided, and the Israelites went through the sea on dry ground, with a wall of water on their right and on their left.

EXODUS 14:10–14, 21–22

Then Jesus came from Galilee to the Jordan to be baptised by John.

MATTHEW 3:13

It was the deadest of dead ends. The Israelites were caught between the devil and the deep blue sea. The 'devil' in this case was the mighty Pharaoh, who had finally released the Israelites from their slavery in Egypt, only to have second thoughts and demand their return. The 'deep blue sea' was an inlet of the Indian Ocean, part of the Great Rift Valley that separates the continents of Africa and Asia.

With Pharaoh and his armies approaching at an alarming speed, the Israelites' response was one of complete panic: first crying out to God (more in desperation than in hope), then rounding on Moses his servant with a series of angry questions. Egypt and the Egyptians: that was the focus of their questioning. Egypt was all they could see, all that they knew; Egypt had been their only reality for 40 years—a brutal reality, true, but at least a familiar one. Yet now their first taste of freedom had turned sour. They had always been suspicious of Moses—suspicious of his privileged upbringing, his rash nature, his madcap schemes; and at this point those suspicions seemed completely justified.

Whatever Moses' inner feelings, his reaction to the situation was both calm and decisive. In response to the Israelites' panic, he spoke of a new approach: 'Do not be afraid', 'Stand firm', 'Only be still'. In response to the terrifying sight of the approaching Egyptian armies he spoke of a new focus: 'See the deliverance the Lord will bring you today'. In response to the sense that there was only one possible outcome to this piece of folly—that the people had been 'brought to the desert to die'—he spoke of a new reality: 'The Lord will fight for you'. This was the same Lord to whom the Israelites had been crying out, of course, but only Moses had truly included him in the equation.

What followed was a miracle of such magnitude, such

awe-inspiring power, that it can variously be understood as the creation, birth and baptism of the people of Israel—their transformation from slavery to freedom, from rabble to nation. As on the third day of creation, when God gathered the water so that dry ground appeared (Genesis 1:9), Moses stretched out his hand over the sea, then led the people through; and having safely negotiated this 'valley of the shadow of death'—the walls of water threatening to engulf them as they later did the Egyptian army—the sense of wonder was almost palpable, finding joyful release in the heartfelt outburst of worship and praise that we'll pick up in tomorrow's reading.

It's not just water that brings together our two readings today, for Jesus' decision to be baptised by John both expressed his oneness with God's ancient people and marked the beginnings of a whole new exodus for Jesus himself and all who would follow him. Expectations were running high that the Messiah was on his way, with the 'devil' now taking the form of Caesar rather than Pharaoh, and with thousands responding to John's call from the desert. Yet from the start Jesus would subvert those expectations, taking on a bigger fish than even the mighty force of Rome. The first exodus brought freedom from the power of Pharaoh and from the daily grinding experience of hardship and humiliation in the life of a slave. This new exodus would bring freedom from the power of death and from the daily grinding experience of guilt and shame in the life of a sinner.

There are many themes we could focus on as we begin our Lenten exodus together. The apostle Paul would tell us of God's presence in the face of the deadest of dead ends: 'God is faithful; he will not let you be tempted beyond what you can bear. But when you are tempted, he will also provide a way out so that you can endure it' (1 Corinthians 10:13).

The early church fathers would remind us that our sins of greed, pride and anger have been drowned in the waters of baptism and need to remain that way. Martin Luther would urge us to practise a faith that grows, not shrinks, in the face of apparently impossible situations, and triumphs as God gloriously intervenes.

Arguably, though, the most helpful challenge of all is simply this: the call, with Moses, to include God in the equation. For whatever the extent of our churchgoing and spiritual maturity—whatever our tendency to cry out into the ether in times of pressure and pain—it remains alarmingly easy to focus on the devil and the deep blue sea and quietly to ignore the powerful, life-giving presence of a God who loves us and who created the universe. 'Do not be afraid.' 'Stand firm.' 'Only be still.' 'The Lord will fight for you.' These are the phrases of an active faith, a faith that enables us to face life calmly, purposefully, trustingly, peacefully; and it is that faith, 'of greater worth than gold' (1 Peter 1:7), that God would wish to refine and strengthen as we travel with the Israelites into the desert and beyond.

A prayer based on Psalm 46

O Lord my God, my refuge and strength, an ever-present help in trouble, grant me stillness and trust, I pray, and fill me afresh with the gladdening presence of your Spirit. Amen

PROVISION
IN THE DESERT

2

THURSDAY: WORSHIP

Then Moses and the Israelites sang this song to the Lord:

'I will sing to the Lord,
for he is highly exalted.
Both horse and driver
he has hurled into the sea.
The Lord is my strength and my defence;
he has become my salvation.
He is my God, and I will praise him,
my father's God, and I will exalt him…
In your unfailing love you will lead
the people you have redeemed.
In your strength you will guide them
to your holy dwelling.'

Then Miriam the prophet, Aaron's sister, took a tambourine in her hand, and all the women followed her, with tambourines and dancing. Miriam sang to them:

'Sing to the Lord,
for he is highly exalted.
Both horse and driver
he has hurled into the sea.'
EXODUS 15:1–2, 13, 20–21

As soon as Jesus was baptised, he went up out of the water. At that moment heaven was opened, and he saw the Spirit of God descending like a dove and alighting on him. And a voice from heaven said, 'This is my Son, whom I love; with him I am well pleased.'
MATTHEW 3:16–17

As the Israelites experienced their first few hours in the desert, they had no idea that they were destined to stay there for a very long time. Had they been quizzed at that point, they would probably have come up with some variation on the theme 'We'll be home for Christmas'.[1] Yet whatever the hardships that lay ahead, the 40 years in the desert would prove both educational and deeply formative. The Lord, through the prophet Hosea, even compared them to the first steps of a much-loved toddler (11:1–4), reminding us of the description of Israel as God's 'firstborn son' in Exodus 4:22.

It must have been deeply encouraging—to the Israelites, to Moses and not least to the Lord himself—that the people's first instinct in those opening hours was to worship: to give glory to God through exuberant singing and dancing, as befitted the child of such an awesome protector and provider. In this 'Song of the Sea' (one of the most ancient hymns in the whole Old Testament), Moses and the people sang of God's power in the face of his enemies, both the forces of Pharaoh and the waters of chaos; and from that place of thankful celebration the message was clear—that the Lord who 'has done' 'will do'; that here was a God they could trust with their very lives and futures.

As we look at the story that lies ahead, it is sad to see just how quickly Israel's worship evaporated, only to be replaced by anxiety, self-centredness and an extraordinary propensity to moan. Only once would Israel recapture the exuberance of these early days, and the object of their worship on that occasion was a golden calf, an idol they'd constructed for themselves. Yet true worship—the ability to lift our eyes heavenwards in thanksgiving and trust—could have proved such an encouraging resource, had the Israelites chosen to exercise it both properly and consistently.

Matthew's Gospel gives us some tiny glimpses into the worship life of Jesus (see, for example, 11:25–27, with its more exuberant parallel in Luke 10:21–22). But while there's no specific reference to Jesus worshipping in the River Jordan, the description of Israel as God's 'firstborn son' is beautifully picked up in the Gospel narrative: 'This is my Son, whom I love; with him I am well pleased.' God loved the Israelites too, of course, and there's little doubt he was 'well pleased' with his son as infant Israel took his first steps in the wilderness: as we read in Hosea, 'To them I was like one who lifts a little child to the cheek, and I bent down to feed them' (11:4). But perhaps the difference between the wilderness experiences of the old Israel and Jesus the new Israel is that the old Israel forgot what it is to worship. To quote from Hosea again (and in an image all too familiar to parents of wilful toddlers!), 'The more they were called, the more they went away from me' (11:2).

The God who 'has done' 'will do': that is a message at the heart of all true worship. It's not a comfortable message or one that guarantees an easy ride: Israel would be led into the wilderness by the pillars of cloud and fire, just as Jesus would be led into the wilderness by the Spirit of God. But in the end it speaks of a world where order triumphs over chaos, and meaning over futility—a world where we can trust in the providence of God even in the midst of threats of the darkest kind.

The simple commitment to let the 'has done' shape the 'will do' may remind us of Paul's confidence that 'he who began a good work in you will carry it on to completion until the day of Christ Jesus' (Philippians 1:6). It may take us back to some words from John Newton's most famous hymn, 'Amazing grace':

Through many dangers, toils and snares
we have already come.
'Twas grace that brought us safe thus far,
and grace will lead us home.

Yet such confidence often proves strangely elusive for Christian believers, just as it did for the people of Israel. The Israelites caught it as they joined with Moses and Miriam in the 'Song of the Sea', yet within days were giving way to a host of anxieties about food, water and their increasingly belligerent desert neighbours. We too can catch it for a while but all too quickly fall back into a default position of faithlessness and fear.

And part of the blessing of regular worship, the ordinary and routine as well as the spontaneous and exuberant, is that it helps us put the 'has done' and the 'will do' together: it reminds us of the 'has done' as we sing and pray, as we study the scriptures and celebrate the Eucharist, and it builds our trust in the 'will do' as we look to a God whose very presence brings order out of chaos.

It's worship that helps make sense of our lives, that reconnects us to our God, that pushes back the chaos as surely as the Lord pushed back the waters of the sea.

A prayer based on Psalm 23:4–6

Lord my Shepherd, I lift to you the shadows in my life, the enemies, the fears. Give me a heart of worship, I pray, that with your presence before me and your goodness and love behind me, I might joyfully walk towards my heavenly home. Amen

3

FRIDAY: HEALING

Then Moses led Israel from the Red Sea and they went into the Desert of Shur. For three days they travelled in the desert without finding water. When they came to Marah, they could not drink its water because it was bitter... So the people grumbled against Moses, saying, 'What are we to drink?' Then Moses cried out to the Lord, and the Lord showed him a piece of wood. He threw it into the water, and the water became sweet. There the Lord made a decree and a law for them, and there he tested them. He said, 'If you listen carefully to the Lord your God and do what is right in his eyes, if you pay attention to his commands and keep all his decrees, I will not bring on you any of the diseases I brought on the Egyptians, for I am the Lord, who heals you.' Then they came to Elim, where there were twelve springs and seventy palm trees, and they camped there near the water.

EXODUS 15:22–27 (NIV)

Then Jesus was led by the Spirit into the wilderness to be tempted by the devil.

MATTHEW 4:1

So far, so good: toddler Israel had experienced a mighty miracle of grace and liberation and had responded with wholehearted worship to her God. As the walk through the desert got properly under way, though, the precarious reality of her situation began to strike home. Three days 'without finding water' must have been an alarming experience even for the best prepared of the Israelite families. Finally coming across Marah, with its plentiful supplies to satisfy themselves and their livestock—only to find the water too bitter to drink —must have come as a terrible disappointment.

In response to a fresh burst of grumbling (one of the more excusable in the long line of Israel's toddler tantrums), Moses threw a piece of wood into the water—from an aromatic shrub, perhaps, whose pungency effectively masked the water's bitterness. A few miles on and the Israelites came to Elim, a genuine oasis whose 'twelve springs and seventy palm trees' brought refreshment of a far more satisfying kind. But it's the verses in between, and especially the striking promise that 'I am the Lord, who heals you', that make this passage unique in the story of Israel's desert wanderings. It's no wonder that the combination of sweetness, healing, shade and refreshment led Welsh preacher George Jeffreys to celebrate this incident when he named his fellowship the 'Elim Pentecostal Church', thus founding one of the most vigorous revival movements of the 20th century.

The Lord's ability to bring disease and destruction had already been displayed in the plagues that had finally forced a reluctant Pharaoh into releasing the Israelites from their slavery in Egypt. Yet this horrible history did not need to be the Israelites' experience. If they remained faithful to God and his commands, they would know him as their healer, not their destroyer, the one who could turn the bitterest of waters into sweetness.

It was a big 'if', of course—the first of many 'ifs' in the

story of the wilderness—and it reveals one side of an on-going tension in the exodus as a whole as to whether God's promises are conditional or unconditional. Certainly, as we shall see, God's choice of Israel in the first place was un-conditional (see Deuteronomy 7:6–8), but even in these early pages of the Bible we can sense the danger of 'cheap grace',[2] of the Israelites taking for granted their privileged position as the people of God.

Forty years later, Moses' successor Joshua was on the verge of capturing the city of Jericho when he had a powerful encounter with an armed angel. 'Are you for us or for our enemies?' asked Joshua, to which the angel remarkably re-sponded, 'Neither, but as commander of the army of the Lord I have now come' (Joshua 5:13–14). And it's that 'neither' that acts as a check against the dark side of being chosen, the tendency (in the church as much as ancient Israel) to assume that however badly we behave, we are, by definition, on the side of the angels.

How would Jesus behave as he left the glory of his baptism and was led, like infant Israel, into the desert? How would he cope with the lack of food and the scarcity of water? Here was a man chosen by God his Father, filled with God's Spirit and anointed to proclaim good news to the poor, freedom for the prisoners, sight for the blind (see Luke 4:18)—a man who perfectly embodied the promise 'I am the Lord, who heals you'. Yet first even Jesus had to go through the toughest of testing, to taste of the waters of Marah, without giving way to the faithlessness and grumbling that characterised his spiritual forebears.

The healing ministry that emerged from those 40 days in the desert would be unconditional and full of grace: there is absolutely no suggestion in the Gospels that Jesus simply healed the good people. But perhaps the conditional clauses in today's first reading have more to say to would-be healers than to those who seek healing.

It's a godly ambition, of course—one that should be universal among all Christian people—the desire to be a 'channel of your peace',[3] an instrument of God's healing and reconciling power to a sick and divided world. Yet today's scriptures remind us that there is no easy journey from the Red Sea to Elim, from baptism to glory: there's no bypass round Marah, no evading the desert, for those who would follow Jesus and seek to be fruitful in his service. Early in Matthew's Gospel (2:11) we hear of three gifts brought to the Christ-child, two of which spoke of kingship and priesthood. The third gift, of course, was myrrh, a bitter resin associated with death and embalming; and it's perhaps no coincidence that 'myrrh' and 'Marah' share the same Hebrew root.

The 'wounded healer'—the person stripped of all pride, all self-centredness and every desire to play to the gallery, to boost his own ratings, to make a name for himself—that is the model of ministry we read of in the story of Jesus. And as the Israelites received the striking revelation by the waters of Marah that 'I am the Lord, who heals you', no one could have conceived of the sacrifice that that apparently simple commitment would one day entail.

A prayer based on Matthew 16:24–27

Jesus, my crucified, risen and exalted Lord, deepen my desire to follow you and my willingness to embrace the cost, for the healing of your world and the blessing of your name. Amen

4

SATURDAY: MANNA

The whole Israelite community set out from Elim and came to the Desert of Sin, which is between Elim and Sinai, on the fifteenth day of the second month after they had come out of Egypt. In the desert the whole community grumbled against Moses and Aaron. The Israelites said to them, 'If only we had died by the Lord's hand in Egypt! There we sat round pots of meat and ate all the food we wanted, but you have brought us out into this desert to starve this entire assembly to death.' Then the Lord said to Moses, 'I will rain down bread from heaven for you. The people are to go out each day and gather enough for that day. In this way I will test them and see whether they will follow my instructions. On the sixth day they are to prepare what they bring in, and that is to be twice as much as they gather on the other days.'

EXODUS 16:1–5

After fasting for forty days and forty nights, he was hungry. The tempter came to him and said, 'If you are the Son of God, tell these stones to become bread.' Jesus answered, 'It is written: "People do not live on bread alone, but on every word that comes from the mouth of God."'

MATTHEW 4:2–4

'What is it?' asked the people of Israel as they analysed a strange flaky substance that had appeared overnight a month after their dramatic departure from the land of Egypt; and it was the Hebrew phrase for 'What is it?' by which the substance soon became known. Many centuries later, in a factory in Corby, some bright employee at the Golden Wonder factory came up with a similar idea when he named the company's latest brand of cheese puffs 'Wotsits', but there the resemblance between the two foodstuffs ends!

What was manna? It comes across as something of a superfood, white like coriander seed and tasting of honey. Various natural explanations have been given of its origins: the tamarisk tree, for example, emits sap in the form of a white flake or ball, which hardens in the sun and tastes sweet with a bread-like consistency when it's gathered in the morning. But there are some aspects of the biblical description that are plainly miraculous.

There was much grumbling during the wanderings in the desert: as has already been noted, the people of Israel could be a grumpy lot, and the complaining at the beginning of today's reading became something of a pattern for the years to come. On this occasion, there are no signs that the Israelites were actually starving. They were simply indulging in a bout of nostalgia, comparing a free but uncertain present with an enslaved yet remarkably rose-tinted past. Even moderately wealthy people in the ancient Near East enjoyed meat on an occasional, not a regular basis. The idea that the Israelite slaves had 'sat round pots of meat' (later embellished with mouth-watering references to fish, cucumbers, melons, leeks, onions and garlic, Numbers 11:5) was quite absurd.

There is a more sympathetic way in which to read this story, of course, in the light of the experience of many others who have made the transition from slavery to freedom. In parts of the former Soviet Union, it's still not unusual to hear the phrase 'We were better off under the communists', just as many ex-prisoners struggle to cope with life on the outside. But Israel was in a much better position than that, moving out from a nation where Pharaoh was Lord into a place of dependence on the great I AM. This new Lord had the power to part the sea itself and to 'rain down bread from heaven' for them. This new Lord had chosen not to enslave but to love, inexplicably hitching his wagon to the people's own. Back in the distant past, one of Israel's ancestors, Esau, had sold his birthright for a bowl of stew, sacrificing his long-term future to gratify an immediate need (Genesis 25:29–34). For Israel to make the same mistake again—to turn her back on Jehovah Jireh (the Lord who provides) and trudge back to her slavery in Egypt—would have been foolish in the extreme.

How could Israel adjust to this new situation, then, to life under her new Lord? How could the people break free from the old habits of anxiety, dishonesty, self-centredness, inequality and hoarding that slavery and imprisonment tend to engender? Only through a period where food would be faithfully provided on a daily basis—the same food for everyone, with quite enough to go round—and where hoarding would be rendered futile through the simple expedient of the superfood's very limited shelf-life. Faith would be further encouraged by commanding the people not to collect manna on the sixth day (the word for 'sabbath' makes its first appearance in the Bible in this chapter) and by miraculously extending its sell-by date by 24 hours on that particular day of the week. Through 40 years of praying, 'Give us today our daily bread' and seeing that prayer daily answered, perhaps the Israelites would be weaned off their experience of the past

400 years, in which lordship had been equated with slavery, bondage, violence and oppression.

Would God provide manna for Jesus as he spent his 40 days in the Judean desert? In the event, it didn't happen, leaving a hungry Jesus with the temptation to do it himself, to 'tell these stones to become bread'. As he reflected on Israel's experience, though—and especially on that great principle from Deuteronomy 8:3, 'People do not live on bread alone but on every word that comes from the mouth of God'— Jesus became convinced that this would be a misuse of his power, an expression of godless self-reliance. Of course he needed food like anyone else, but above all he needed God's word, God's direction, as his first and overriding priority. 'My food,' as he later put it, 'is to do the will of him who sent me and to finish his work' (John 4:34).

We, like the Israelites, need to be weaned off an unhealthy self-reliance and our natural tendency towards anxiety, dishonesty, self-centredness, inequality and hoarding. It's perhaps for that reason that almost every Christian is called at times to endure 'grief in all kinds of trials' (1 Peter 1:6), with the control of our career and finances, children and relationships, health and future somehow wrested from us. Such experiences, however painful, can be of life-changing significance, reminding us once again of our dependence on God and the trust that goes with it. At such times it may take all our faith simply to hang on in there, but hang on in there we must. For 'these [trials] have come so that your faith... may be proved genuine and may result in praise, glory and honour when Jesus Christ is revealed' (1 Peter 1:7).

A prayer based on John 6:35, 68

Lord Jesus, living bread, feed, sustain and nourish me all my journey through, for you have the words of eternal life and in your service is perfect freedom. Amen

5

SUNDAY: WATER

The whole Israelite community set out from the Desert of Sin, travelling from place to place as the Lord commanded. They camped at Rephidim, but there was no water for the people to drink. So they quarrelled with Moses and said, 'Give us water to drink.' Moses replied, 'Why do you quarrel with me? Why do you put the Lord to the test?' But the people were thirsty for water there, and they grumbled against Moses. They said, 'Why did you bring us up out of Egypt to make us and our children and livestock die of thirst?' Then Moses cried out to the Lord, 'What am I to do with these people? They are almost ready to stone me.' The Lord answered Moses, 'Go out in front of the people. Take with you some of the elders of Israel and take in your hand the staff with which you struck the Nile, and go. I will stand there before you by the rock at Horeb. Strike the rock, and water will come out of it for the people to drink.' So Moses did this in the sight of the elders of Israel. And he called the place Massah and Meribah because the Israelites quarrelled and because they tested the Lord saying, 'Is the Lord among us or not?'

EXODUS 17:1–7

Then the devil took him to the holy city and had him stand on the highest point of the temple. 'If you are the Son of

God,' he said, 'throw yourself down. For it is written: "He will command his angels concerning you, and they will lift you up in their hands, so that you will not strike your foot against a stone."' Jesus answered him, 'It is also written: "Do not put the Lord your God to the test."'

MATTHEW 4:5–7

Despite the regular supply of manna (soon supplemented by a flock of quails, which arrived in unimaginable numbers to answer the people's craving for meat), there remained another obvious need in the desert once the Israelites struck out from the twelve springs at Elim (15:27). Water again was in short supply, and it wasn't long before Moses faced a second angry delegation, complete with the mutinous grumbling that was becoming something of a trademark of the people of God.

On one level we can understand those grumbles better than the rose-tinted nostalgia of Exodus 16. The people needed water—so did their children and cattle—and at least there was no mention made of the pomegranate juice they'd enjoyed in Egypt or the vintage red they'd sipped by the side of the Nile! But there's an ugliness about today's reading that is new and unsettling. It's not simply that Moses felt in real danger of losing his life at the hands of his own people. It's also that the legitimate language of 'asking' was being replaced by the quite illegitimate language of demanding and manipulation.

There is all the difference in the world, of course, between asking and demanding, for one assumes a position of proper respect, the other a position of unjustified superiority. Two children wait at the checkout counter of a supermarket. One child politely asks for sweets; the other child demands them. Both may get their way but the two transactions could hardly be more different. The first is characterised by gratitude and grace, the second by harassment and humiliation. It's no wonder that we use the same word, 'spoilt', to refer to indulged children and to goods that have been damaged in transit.

Israel had been spoilt at Massah, spoilt most of all by their pathetic attempt to manipulate God. 'Is the Lord among us or not?' they had asked, with the clear implication that unless God did what they demanded, they would simply stop believing in him. Jesus recognised just the same temptation during his 40 days in the wilderness: the appeal (in the words of his quotation from Deuteronomy 6:16) of putting God to the test, of telling God what to do, or else... On the face of it, the idea of a spectacular stunt—jumping off the top of the temple, say—had its attractions. It chimed in nicely with Malachi's prophecy, 'Suddenly the Lord will come to his temple' (3:1: you could hardly get more sudden than that!) and with the promise in Psalm 91:12 that 'you will not strike your foot against a stone'. Yet Jesus' destiny was not as a spoilt child but as a beloved son with whom 'I am well pleased' (Matthew 3:17). Plenty of miracles would be performed, but never for the sake of enhancing his own reputation or seeking to twist God's arm.

It's easy to see temptation as an inward urge to do something wrong, to commit a sin of one kind or another. We are tempted, perhaps, to defraud the tax man or cheat on our marriage partner or (at a somewhat more mundane level) buy a particularly luscious cream cake, whose chocolate coating and creamy interior will set back the diet by a couple of weeks. But when it comes to the story of Massah and to the second of Jesus' temptations, the problem is not an action but an attitude. It is not wrong to ask for water. It is not wrong (though in our case it would be extremely foolish) to perform a spectacular stunt like jumping off the top of the Jerusalem temple. The temptation in both situations is to put God to the test, to assume a position of assertive manipulation rather than one of proper respect. From the garden of Eden onwards, the key question has always been the same: not just 'How can I resist temptation?' but rather 'Who's the boss?'

Respect is a somewhat old-fashioned virtue in a world increasingly distrustful of human hierarchy. In every walk of life there is now an expectation that respect must be earned rather than belonging (as of right) to a particular office or calling. At best this is a positive development, a natural extension of the democratic ideal, flushing out the corrupt and the incompetent, the arrogant and the self-serving. At worst it leads to quite unrealistic expectations being laid on public figures and to a culture of suspicion, disobedience, cynicism and anarchy.

Brought up in this culture of disrespect, it is all too easy for today's worshippers to incorporate such a tendency into our life with God himself—to stop regarding God as worthy of our worship simply because of who he is, and to start offering conditional worship instead on the basis of what he does for us. We become like spoilt children, coming before our heavenly Father with demands, not requests; or else (in the graphic image of the prophet Isaiah), like clay pots that dare to question the skill of their Maker (45:9). Far better the approach of Shadrach, Meshach and Abednego, the friends of Daniel, who resolutely refused to put God to the test, even as they stood before a burning fiery furnace: 'If we are thrown into the blazing furnace, the God we serve is able to save us from it, and he will rescue us from your hand, O king. But even if he does not, we want you to know, O king, that we will not serve your gods or worship the image of gold you have set up' (Daniel 3:17–18, NIV).

A prayer, based on Isaiah 45:5, 9–10

You are the Lord, and there is no other. You are my Maker, my Saviour, my Father. Take this clay that you have made, soften it and mould it into something useful for your purposes, for your glory's sake. Amen

6

MONDAY: PROTECTION

The Amalekites came and attacked the Israelites at Rephidim. Moses said to Joshua, 'Choose some of our men and go out to fight the Amalekites. Tomorrow I will stand on top of the hill with the staff of God in my hands.' So Joshua fought the Amalekites as Moses had ordered, and Moses, Aaron and Hur went to the top of the hill. As long as Moses held up his hands, the Israelites were winning, but whenever he lowered his hands, the Amalekites were winning. When Moses' hands grew tired, they took a stone and put it under him and he sat on it. Aaron and Hur held his hands up—one on one side, one on the other—so that his hands remained steady till sunset. So Joshua overcame the Amalekite army with the sword... Moses built an altar and called it The Lord is my Banner.

EXODUS 17:8–13, 15

Again, the devil took him to a very high mountain and showed him all the kingdoms of the world and their splendour. 'All this I will give you,' he said, 'if you will bow down and worship me.' Jesus said to him, 'Away from me, Satan! For it is written: "Worship the Lord your God, and serve him only."' Then the devil left him, and angels came and attended him.

MATTHEW 4:8–11

Manna, quail and water could well supply the physical appetites of the people of Israel, but it wasn't long before a new need emerged as their presence began to attract the unwelcome attentions of a tribal grouping known as the Amalekites. We can understand the Amalekites' concern at this point. Eking out a livelihood in the Sinai peninsula was already a fairly precarious activity, and the thought of having to share their limited resources with another 600,000 people was a worrying one, even given the rumours of bread and meat raining down from heaven and water emerging from rocks. But the Amalekites' response to the situation was both cruel and uncalled-for. According to the report of their activities in Deuteronomy 25:18, 'When you were weary and worn out, they met you on your journey and cut off all who were lagging behind; they had no fear of God' (NIV). And it was particularly this strategy of cutting off 'those who were lagging behind' (a tactic the Amalekites shared with leopards, lions and bullies everywhere) that most angered a compassionate God, earning for the Amalekites an unenviable reputation that was to dog them for generations to come.

From small, focused attacks on the weak and vulnerable, the Amalekites were eventually able to mount a more concerted campaign against a nation that massively outnumbered them but was not remotely organised in a military sense; and it's at this point that Joshua makes his first appearance in the biblical story. We are not told just how the Israelites managed to assemble a fighting force or how many weapons they had to fight with, but Exodus 17 records the first of many battles the Israelites were to win with Joshua at the helm. A stone altar was built to commemorate the occasion and was given the name 'The Lord is my Banner'.

The most striking part of today's story, though, is not the

battle itself but the sight of an old man holding up his hands on the top of a hill, with two other men propping him up on either side. Commentators have come up with a number of suggestions of what Moses was actually doing: some of them have even regarded his activities as a kind of primitive semaphore for directing the battle, as practised by many a manager on the sidelines of a football match! But the way the story is told suggests rather that Moses was praying to the Lord on the mountain as Joshua fought with the Amalekites in the valley. In the words of the psalmist, 'Hear my cry for mercy as I call to you for help, as I lift up my hands towards your Most Holy Place' (28:2).

Assuming this explanation to be the right one, here was another foundation stone in the early education of the Israelites—that God would protect them from their enemies (especially those as heartless as the Amalekites), but only as they prayed and interceded before him. Victory on the battlefield was not guaranteed simply because they were the people of God. Once the hands were lowered—once the intercession ceased—it was the Amalekites, not the Israelites, who would have the upper hand.

It's much the same lesson that lay behind Jesus' third temptation in the wilderness: an invitation metaphorically to lower his hands (even to raise them to another 'god') in order to achieve the most universal of human victories. It's not that Satan's offer was completely hollow. The promise 'All this I will give you' fits neatly with God's ultimate plan that 'every knee should bow... and every tongue confess that Jesus Christ is Lord' (Philippians 2:10–11, NIV). But despite this broadside at his weakest point (as if Satan had learnt a thing or two from the Amalekites), Jesus quickly saw through the scheme, courageously quoting that foundational text from Deuteronomy 6:13: 'Worship the Lord and serve him only'. 'What good will it be for a man', as he later put it, 'if he gains the whole world, yet forfeits his soul?' (Matthew 16:26, NIV).

The image of a man standing on a hill, with another man on either side of him, brings to mind the story of Jesus' transfiguration, where it was Moses and Elijah who supported Jesus as he looked ahead to the events of the first Good Friday (indeed, Luke at this point speaks of Jesus' 'exodus', which he was to 'bring to fulfilment at Jerusalem', 9:31). It also evokes that darker image on Mount Calvary, as Jesus, hanging between two thieves, continued resisting the temptation to 'lower his hands' to the end (see Matthew 27:40). And for us too, as followers of this 'Prince of Peace', it remains a powerful and inspiring picture.

Yes, there's work to be done: there's a spiritual battle to be fought in the valley as we seek to make the most of our life here on earth. But even the best we can do will only achieve lasting fruit as we also spend time on the mountain, joining with the psalmist in his commitment to praise God as long as we live, and lift up our hands in his name (see Psalm 63:4). And when we're too old or infirm to join Joshua in the valley, the call to join Moses on the mountain—to worship God and pray for others in the thick of the battle—becomes still more urgent. Like Moses, we may need to sit down more than we used to and depend on others for our physical support, but our role is still indispensable. No one is redundant in the kingdom of God.

A prayer based on Psalm 63

Lord, earnestly I seek you; I thirst for you in a dry and parched land where there is no water. Because your love is better than life, I will praise you and lift up my hands in your name. Protect me from all harm this day, and keep me under the shadow of your wing. Amen

7

TUESDAY: LEADERSHIP

Now Jethro, the priest of Midian and father-in-law of Moses, heard of everything God had done for Moses and for his people Israel, and how the Lord had brought Israel out of Egypt... Jethro was delighted to hear about all the good things the Lord had done for Israel in rescuing them from the hand of the Egyptians... The next day Moses took his seat to serve as judge for the people, and they stood around him from morning till evening. When his father-in-law saw all that Moses was doing for the people, he said, 'What is this you are doing for the people? Why do you alone sit as judge, while all these people stand round you from morning till evening?' Moses answered him, 'Because the people come to me to seek God's will. Whenever they have a dispute, it is brought to me, and I decide between the parties and inform them of God's decrees and instructions.'

Moses' father-in-law replied, 'What you are doing is not good. You and these people who come to you will only wear yourselves out. The work is too heavy for you; you cannot handle it alone... Select capable men from all the people— men who fear God, trustworthy men who hate dishonest gain—and appoint them as officials over thousands, hundreds, fifties and tens. Have them serve as judges for the people at all times, but have them bring every difficult case to you; the simple cases they can decide themselves.

That will make your load lighter, because they will share it with you.'

EXODUS 18:1, 9, 13–18, 21–22

As Jesus was walking beside the Sea of Galilee, he saw two brothers, Simon called Peter and his brother Andrew. They were casting a net into the lake, for they were fishermen. 'Come, follow me,' Jesus said, 'and I will send you out to fish for people.' At once they left their nets and followed him.

MATTHEW 4:18–20

The exodus had begun; the Red Sea had parted; the people of Israel had experienced God's physical provision; their first military victory had been secured under Joshua and beneath the upraised arms of Moses; and Exodus 18 gives us a chance to pause a little, to reflect on the extraordinary story so far and begin to look to Mount Sinai and beyond.

The appearance of Jethro, Moses' father-in-law, on the scene takes us right back to the early chapters in the book of Exodus and to the 40 years Moses spent as a refugee in the land of Midian. During that time he was housed by Jethro, worked for him and ended up marrying his daughter Zipporah (Exodus 2:11–22). Much water had flowed under the bridge (and out of the rock!) since then. Zipporah and their two boys had been sent back to Midian, probably to keep them safe through all the upheaval of the exodus. And Jethro's arrival, with Moses' wife and boys in tow (18:5), was a loving and joyous affair, complete with greeting, kissing and (we presume) as slap-up a meal as could be arranged, given the limited range of ingredients on offer!

It is always good to be able to tell our story to a gracious listener: the experiences of being listened to and of being loved are so close as to be virtually indistinguishable from one another; and there's no question that Jethro listened well, catching Moses' enthusiasm and responding with wonder and delight. Scholars have debated what kind of faith Jethro, the 'priest of Midian', held up to this point, but having heard about 'all the good things the Lord had done', he was at least able to acknowledge that 'the Lord is greater than all other gods' (v. 11).

Jethro wasn't simply a good listener, though. As he witnessed Moses at work the following day, he was shocked to find his son-in-law engaged from morning to night in adjudicating a hundred petty disputes—work that, as Jethro was quick to point out, was both wearying for Moses and deeply frustrating for the waiting crowds. In the first two chapters of the Bible we read how everything that God made was 'good', 'good' and 'very good'; and it therefore comes as something of a shock when we come across the first 'not good' of scripture: 'It is not good for the man to be alone' (Genesis 2:18). The second 'not good' of scripture is spoken by Jethro, not God, in response to Moses' punishing schedule, but it shares certain similarities with the Lord's concern in the garden of Eden. It was 'not good' for Moses to be alone. Moses needed to 'select capable men' and share his workload, so that he could concentrate on the more complex cases and justice could be carried out with the greatest speed and efficiency.

Jethro's common sense, which led to the development of a leadership structure built along military lines, has rightly been celebrated as an object lesson in the art of delegation. In all the euphoria of their escape from Egypt, the Israelites had required a style of leadership that was courageous and charismatic; but looking ahead, there was a complementary need for proper organisation if the divine principles of freedom, fairness and justice were truly to be fleshed out in the everyday lives of God's people. Good leadership requires good leaders (and Moses was certainly one of those), but it also requires a good leadership structure. And the fact that *Israel's* leadership structure came not through divine revelation but through human common sense—indeed, the common sense of a pagan priest—must rank as one of the most radical features of the book of Exodus, reminding us that such wisdom is often to be found outside, not within, the confines of the walls of the church.

As he emerged from the desert to begin his public ministry, Jesus recognised the need to call others to share in his mission, and the fact that the Church of Christ now numbers an estimated 2.1 billion people from almost every 'nation, tribe, people and language' (Revelation 7:9) demonstrates the extraordinary effectiveness of his leadership strategy. The Bible teaches us that good leadership is part of God's provision for his people and that leaders are to be held in the greatest respect 'as those who must give an account' (Hebrews 13:17). We are to obey our leaders, to pray for them and to aspire to leadership if that is God's calling on our lives (see Romans 13:1–5; 1 Timothy 2:1–2; 3:1). In Moses himself, Israel was blessed with a leader of courage, faith and humility. Through Jethro she was blessed with a model of shared leadership based on faithfulness to God and personal integrity, which would set her in excellent stead for generations to come.

A prayer based on Hebrews 13:17

Thank you, Father, for those who keep watch over us as those who are accountable to you alone. Bless them, encourage them and give them the respect of those they lead, that their work might be a joy, not a burden, for Jesus' sake. Amen

8

WEDNESDAY: VISION

Then Moses went up to God, and the Lord called to him from the mountain and said, 'This is what you are to say to the house of Jacob and what you are to tell the people of Israel: "You yourselves have seen what I did to Egypt, and how I carried you on eagles' wings and brought you to myself. Now if you obey me fully and keep my covenant, then out of all nations you will be my treasured possession. Although the whole earth is mine, you will be for me a kingdom of priests and a holy nation." These are the words you are to speak to the Israelites.'

EXODUS 19:3–6

Now when Jesus saw the crowds, he went up on a mountainside and sat down. His disciples came to him, and he began to teach them.

MATTHEW 5:1–2

In any biblical word association game, the word 'mountain' should immediately bring to mind the related word 'vision'. Two mountains in particular, Mount Sinai (also known as 'Horeb') and Mount Zion, play a central role in God's purposes, and other mountains—Nebo, Carmel and the Mount of Olives—also take an honoured place in the history of salvation alongside the unnamed locations for the Sermon on the Mount and the transfiguration (traditionally assumed to be Mount Tabor). In his encounter with the woman of Samaria, Jesus emphasised that the worship of God was not restricted to any particular mountain but that true worshippers 'worship the Father in spirit and truth' (John 4:21–23, NIV); yet the psalmist still expresses the feelings of many an enthusiastic fell-walker as he exclaims, 'I will lift up mine eyes unto the hills, from whence cometh my help' (Psalm 121:1, KJV).

Three great biblical characters—Moses, Elijah and Jesus himself—seem to have been especially drawn to the heights, and it's perhaps no coincidence that their only recorded meeting took place on a mountain (Luke 9:31). It's partly that mountains offer the precious gift of solitude; it's partly that they speak of the majesty of God, the One who himself is 'high and lifted up' (Isaiah 6:1); but perhaps, too, it was the view from the top—the bigger picture, the wider vision— that frequently attracted these three spiritual giants on to the slopes. Not that the view from Mount Sinai was particularly panoramic in Exodus 19, covered as it was by smoke and thick cloud.

In his previous visit to Mount Sinai (or Horeb), Moses was famously called to 'take off your sandals, for the place where you are standing is holy ground' (Exodus 3:5). It was during that encounter at the burning bush that Moses received both a fresh vision of the Lord himself and a fresh (and somewhat alarming) vision of his own pivotal role in God's plan of salvation. 'When you have brought the people out of Egypt', the Lord had said on that occasion, 'you will worship God on this mountain' (v. 12); and now that had happened, with the first leg of the exodus adventure successfully accomplished.

Moses had already reflected on the story thus far with

Jethro his father-in-law, but the arrival at Mount Sinai was a time for the Israelites as a whole to reflect on the extraordinary events of the past few months. A fresh vision of God himself came to mind—the Lord as a great and majestic eagle, gently nurturing his fledglings and bringing them safely home. A fresh vision of Israel's pivotal role in God's plan of salvation—as a 'treasured possession', yes, but also a 'kingdom of priests and a holy nation'—was a further part of the picture. If they obeyed God fully and kept his covenant, Israel would have unique access to God as a kingdom of priests, and a unique calling as a holy nation—all lived out against the backdrop of God's promises to Abraham (Genesis 12:1–3) and his continuing care for the whole of his creation.

As Jesus went up on a mountainside to deliver his Sermon on the Mount, he took the role of all three participants in the Sinai drama: the role of Israel, God's 'treasured possession'; the role of Moses, Israel's prophet and teacher; and even the role of the Lord himself, with the authoritative phrase 'I tell you' repeated 14 times in just three chapters. Given previous associations, we would expect this mountain sermon to impart a fresh vision of God and of his calling on his people, and that is precisely what it does. God is revealed as 'our Father' for the first time in Matthew's Gospel, and Jesus' radical teaching presents the perfect model of what it is to live as citizens of the kingdom of God.

The word 'vision' has long been detached from its relationship to mountains and, indeed, from its spiritual moorings. Almost every school, business, charity and political party now has a so-called 'vision statement', setting out the aims of the organisation, its ethos and what it hopes to achieve in the coming years. 'Vision' has therefore come to mean little more than a set of good ideas based on round-table discussions and future forecasting, culminating in the production of a glossy document, complete with colourful pictures of smiling employees and glowing testimonials from satisfied customers.

There is, of course, some value in this exercise for schools and businesses and, indeed, for churches as we seek to focus our efforts to best effect. But there is a danger, even in Christian circles, that the 'v' word becomes robbed of its spiritual significance and thereby of its power to bless and inspire. How encouraging for the Israelites in the wilderness to catch a fresh vision of God as a mighty desert eagle and of themselves as his 'treasured possession', a kingdom of priests and a holy nation. What a blessing for us, too, to be refreshed and renewed in our vision of God and to reflect on our own calling as a 'chosen people, a royal priesthood, a holy nation, God's special possession, that [we] may declare the praises of him who called [us] out of darkness into his wonderful light' (1 Peter 2:9).

And if we've lost that sense of the majesty of God and that bigger picture of what he is calling us to do, perhaps it's time to climb a mountain.

A prayer based on Isaiah 40:28–31

Everlasting God, Creator of the ends of the earth, whose understanding no one can fathom, may I lift up my eyes today to behold your glory; may I rise on eagles' wings as I put my hope in you. Amen

9

THURSDAY: LAW

And God spoke all these words: 'I am the Lord your God, who brought you out of Egypt, out of the land of slavery. You shall have no other gods before me. You shall not make for yourself an image in the form of anything in heaven above or on the earth beneath or in the waters below... You shall not misuse the name of the Lord your God... Remember the Sabbath day by keeping it holy... Honour your father and your mother... You shall not murder. You shall not commit adultery. You shall not steal. You shall not give false testimony against your neighbour. You shall not covet...'

EXODUS 20:1–4, 7–8, 12–17 (ABRIDGED)

'Do not think that I have come to abolish the Law or the Prophets; I have not come to abolish them but to fulfil them... For I tell you that unless your righteousness surpasses that of the Pharisees and the teachers of the law, you will certainly not enter the kingdom of heaven.'

MATTHEW 5:17, 20

Stark, simple, comprehensive: the Ten Commandments (or 'ten words', as the Israelites came to know them) are properly seen as the very foundation of the Jewish Law and of all later legal systems based on Judeo-Christian values. It is not unusual today to enter a church and find the Ten Commandments displayed on a wall in the chancel, sometimes neatly paired with the Lord's Prayer on the opposite side. Meanwhile, battles continue in the United States as to whether or not the posting of the Commandments on public buildings (many of them dating back to 1956, when Cecil B. DeMille erected hundreds of tablets as a stunt to promote his film *The Ten Commandments*) is an infringement of the First Amendment to the US Constitution.

Just as the Israelites needed a leadership structure as they began to consolidate their life as a nation, so too they needed a robust legal code, and the giving of the Law in the desert was, in part, God's gracious provision for the peace and well-being of his people. Behind it, though, lay a sense of warning, even threat. The smoke and trumpet blasts, the thunder and lightning all acted as reminders that you messed with this God at your peril, that to be his covenant people was both an awesome privilege and an extraordinary responsibility. No reason was communicated as to why these commandments were important; no exceptions were allowed, and no room given over to discussion or debate. Instead, a series of 'Thou shalts' and 'Thou shalt not's was simply issued by God from out of the fire on the mountain.

It is not difficult to see the universal relevance of the last six commandments for the growth of a healthy society. The Hebrew word for 'honouring' your father and mother (the fifth commandment) means literally 'giving proper weight' to their feelings and needs. The Hebrew word for 'coveting' your neighbour's house, wife 'or anything that belongs to your neighbour' (the tenth commandment) speaks of both an inner acquisitiveness and its outworking in terms of plots and scheming (the story of David, Bathsheba and poor Uriah the Hittite being a particularly nasty case in point: see 2 Samuel 11). There may be some debate about what exactly constitutes unlawful killing and of how far sexual misconduct should be criminalised, but overall, we might conclude, the last six commandments ('loving your neighbour as yourself', in Jesus' neat summary: Matthew 22:39) would not look out of place on the most secular of public buildings, whether put up there by Christian activists, Cecil B. DeMille or anyone else.

If 'loving your neighbour as yourself' remains fashionable (in theory, at least), quite the opposite applies to loving 'the Lord your God with all your heart and with all your soul and with all your mind' (Matthew 22:37). Commandments one to three forbid the worship of other gods, the portrayal of God in any earthly form and the taking of his name in vain— every attempt, in fact, to domesticate God, to tame him or to neutralise his sole authority by setting him up as just one among many. Meanwhile, commandment number four stipulates that a whole day a week is to be dedicated to this God, given over to rest, just as God himself rested. Beyond the recognised need for regular time off, not one of these first four commandments makes any kind of sense within a secular framework.

How, then, do Christians stand when it comes to the Ten Commandments?

First and foremost, we know that we are saved by God's grace and not by meticulously ticking the legalistic boxes. In one startling passage, the writer to the Hebrews contrasts Mount Sinai with Mount Zion, setting the 'darkness, gloom and storm' of the old covenant against the joy, light and perfection of the new (12:18–24).

Yet the Ten Commandments still have a central place

both in Jesus' teaching and in the life of the Christian believer. In his ministry Jesus regularly drew his followers back to the heart of the commandments, both teaching and embodying a life of love rather than a tick-box legalism; and his references to murder and adultery (the sixth and seventh commandments) in the Sermon on the Mount show how this thinking worked, allowing God's Law to search our inner hearts, not just to judge our outward actions (Matthew 5:21–22). For Jesus, as for Moses, the idea that you could separate the last six commandments from the first four was quite unthinkable—and here is an argument that Christians need to take to those who oppose any kind of religion, considering it a negative influence. It's quite possible, of course, to be an unbeliever and a good person (or, indeed, a believer and a bad person), but the evidence of a link between, say, growing godlessness in a society and the incidence of family breakdown is not exactly hard to find.

It was an ex-offender who cast fresh light for me on the Ten Commandments. Coming to the end of a long prison sentence, during which he'd become a Christian, this man was fearful of what would happen when he finally left the confines of his prison cell. Would he be able to keep it up? Would he simply revert to a life of crime, as so many of his contemporaries had done? On entering a church, where the commandments were clearly displayed, this man found himself reading them as promises, not demands: 'You *shall* not murder. You *shall* not commit adultery. You *shall* not steal.' By God's grace, and in the power of his Spirit, this new life was at last a glorious possibility—and hearing the man retell the story five years later was a joy and privilege, a reminder of the continuing power of the word of God and the Spirit of God to inspire faith, hope and transformation.

A prayer based on Jeremiah 31:33

Lord Almighty, take your law and write it on my heart today, that I might know, love and serve you from the overflow of your presence within me, for Jesus' sake. Amen

10

FRIDAY: BEAUTY

Then the Lord said to Moses, 'See, I have chosen Bezalel son of Uri, the son of Hur, of the tribe of Judah, and I have filled him with the Spirit of God, with wisdom, with understanding, with knowledge and with all kinds of skills—to make artistic designs for work in gold, silver and bronze, to cut and set stones, to work in wood, and to engage in all kinds of crafts.'
EXODUS 31:1–5

'Why do you worry about clothes? See how the flowers of the field grow. They do not labour or spin. Yet I tell you that not even Solomon in all his splendour was dressed like one of these.'
MATTHEW 6:28–29

'You shall not make for yourself an idol,' thundered the Lord from Mount Sinai, and for a moment it looked as if Israel's craftsmen might be out of a job—the later fate of the idol makers of Ephesus in response to the dynamic preaching of Paul (Acts 19:23–27). But the prohibition against the making of idols was in no way an attack on the arts. Rather, it demonstrated a humble recognition that nothing created by a human craftsman could possibly capture the character and glory of God himself.

There is a strand of Christian tradition that celebrates the grey, creating the plainest of church buildings and the dullest of musical chants so as to avoid any inadvertent breach of the second commandment; but that was never God's plan from the beginning. The very fact that it was on Mount Sinai itself that the Lord passed on his plans for the tabernacle, with its rich furnishings of gold, silver and bronze, blue, purple and scarlet yarn, acacia wood and onyx stones, suggests that the worship of Yahweh was hardly intended to be a drab and colourless affair.

The Lord himself, of course, is the supreme craftsman, and Jesus' reference to the 'flowers of the field'—the crocuses, anemones and gladioli that grow in great profusion in the rich Galilean soil—was both warm and appreciative of his Father's imagination and care: 'not even Solomon in all his splendour was dressed like one of these'. Yet the Lord has imparted some measure of that creativity to those made in his image, too.

Bezalel was one such person: his name means 'in God's shadow' and his artistry and craftsmanship were literally inspired, as the Lord promised to fill him with 'the Spirit of God, with wisdom, with understanding, with knowledge and with all kind of skills'. He was soon joined by an assistant called Oholiab, and 13 of the last 16 chapters in the book of Exodus are preoccupied with the work they were called to do. First God passed on his blueprint for the ark of the covenant, the table and lampstand, the tabernacle, the altars, the 'courtyard', the oil and the priestly garments (chs. 25—31); next, Bezalel and Oholiab got to work, skilfully constructing the tabernacle and its furnishings out of materials donated by the whole Israelite community (chs. 35—40). The Lord passed on the basic materials and plans but there was still room for Bezalel and Oholiab to create and improvise, 'to make artistic designs for work in gold, silver and bronze'. There may even be a parallel here to the Sinai view of discipleship, where the giving of the Law—the setting of the basic parameters for our lives—still allows room for individuality, creativity and improvisation, for being filled and led by the Spirit of God.

For Christian artists and craftspeople everywhere (and scientists and engineers, too), today's reading should act as a real encouragement. We are used to the lists of spiritual gifts in Paul's letters—the set in 1 Corinthians 12, for example, which includes wisdom, knowledge, faith, healing, miraculous powers, prophecy and so on—but the story of Bezalel speaks of human creativity as a further gift of the Spirit, with skilled metalworkers, woodworkers and jewellers all reflecting a God-given wisdom and knowledge as they go about their work. We have already been treated to inspiring poetry and music in the desert, to noisy tambourines and exuberant dancing (Exodus 15:1–21). Now it is the turn of the visual arts—arts which (like all good gifts) can be abused when they stray beyond their divinely ordained limits but which remain a source of great blessing, challenge, encouragement and joy when placed at the service of the Creator and those made in his image.

Why, though, are quite so many chapters of the Bible devoted to the construction of the tabernacle and its furnishings? The main reason is that the tabernacle was to be the symbolic connection between Mount Sinai and the coming temple, the place where the presence of God was located or heightened during those wilderness years and their aftermath. Yet perhaps, too, these chapters contain an acknowledgment of the human need for beauty, for creativity, for colour and vibrancy during our time in the desert. And for today's urban-dwellers in particular—those who look out over concrete and tarmac, with streetlamps obscuring the light of the stars—there is a special need to attend to these matters, to feed the soul, if life is to be enriched and inspiring. Some of the best pioneers of inner-city ministry from the 19th century onwards have responded to that need by filling their churches with life and colour (and organising regular trips to the seaside); and when we are feeling somehow out of sorts with the world around us, it could be that the Lord might prescribe a walk in the country, a trip to an art gallery or listening to a particularly inspiring CD, rather than simply (as we might imagine) pointing to the poverty of our discipleship or the indiscipline of our prayer life.

A prayer based on Psalm 24

Praise you, Lord, that the earth is yours, and everything in it. Praise you for the awesome beauty of all that you have made and for the gift of creativity passed on to those made in your image. Give me clean hands and a pure heart—come and dwell within me in the fullness of your Spirit—that I might use all that I am and all that I have to bring glory to your name. Amen

11

SATURDAY: FALL

When the people saw that Moses was so long in coming down from the mountain, they gathered around Aaron and said, 'Come, make us gods who will go before us. As for this fellow Moses who brought us up out of Egypt, we don't know what has happened to him.' Aaron answered them, 'Take off the gold earrings that your wives, your sons and your daughters are wearing, and bring them to me.' So all the people took off their earrings and brought them to Aaron. He took what they handed him and made it into an idol cast in the shape of a calf, fashioning it with a tool. Then they said, 'These are your gods, Israel, who brought you up out of Egypt.' When Aaron saw this, he built an altar in front of the calf and announced, 'Tomorrow there will be a festival to the Lord.' So the next day the people rose early and sacrificed burnt offerings and presented fellowship offerings. Afterward they sat down to eat and drink and got up to indulge in revelry.

EXODUS 32:1–6

'No one can serve two masters. Either you will hate the one and love the other, or you will be devoted to the one and despise the other. You cannot serve both God and Money.'

MATTHEW 6:24

If the parting of the Red Sea marked Israel's creation, birth and baptism, the incident of the golden calf marks her fall. In the garden of Eden, Adam and Eve had specifically been told, 'You must not eat from the tree of the knowledge of good and evil' (Genesis 2:17); at Mount Sinai the Israelites had specifically been told, 'You shall have no other gods before me' and 'You shall not make yourself an idol' (Exodus 20: 3–4, NIV). Yet in each respective case the instruction was hardly out of the Lord's mouth before the fruit was eaten and the idol built. Eve and Aaron even shared a common tendency to shift the blame on to everyone except themselves.

Impatience was the Israelites' motivation (or, at least, their excuse) in coming to Aaron with their demands. Moses— here described both roughly and rudely as 'this fellow... who brought us up out of Egypt'—had been gone for 40 days and there was no knowing when or even whether he would return. Meanwhile, the Israelites were digesting the Ten Commandments without the aid of their leader and foremost prophet, and Aaron (their deputy leader and lesser prophet) was being measured up for his 'sacred garments... to give him dignity and honour' (Exodus 28:2), a time fraught with spiritual danger for even the humblest of individuals.

Just as, in later years, the people would come before the prophet Samuel with the demand, 'We want a king over us. Then we shall be like all the other nations' (1 Samuel 8: 19–20), so the people now came to Aaron, demanding 'gods', idols, so that they too would be like the other nations, the Egyptians and the Canaanite tribes around them. The idea of a God who couldn't be pictured or carved or moulded had been clearly presented to them just days before. Yet perhaps it was simply too radical a concept for the people (and even, it seems, for Aaron) to contemplate.

And so we are witnesses to a dark parody of the earlier events on Mount Sinai, where the people present their offerings, craftsmen are appointed, altars are built, sacrifices offered and feast days announced, and where the golden calf is celebrated with the words 'These are your gods, Israel, who brought you up out of Egypt'—a terrible distortion of the words that preceded the giving of the Ten Commandments, 'I am the Lord your God, who brought you out of Egypt, out of the land of slavery' (Exodus 20:2). Following the gift of the Law, Moses, Aaron and the 'leaders of Israel' had been granted an extraordinary vision on the mountain where they 'saw God, and they ate and drank' (24:11). In the parody, we read of more eating and drinking—but in place of the words 'they saw God' we are told that they 'got up to indulge in revelry', a Hebrew euphemism for debauchery and sexual excess.

'No one can serve two masters,' taught Jesus in his Sermon on the Mount, and as a commentary on the incident of the golden calf it could hardly be bettered. A covenant relationship with God (as, indeed, with a marriage partner) must by its nature be exclusive if it is truly to prosper and thrive.

As so often, though, Jesus' teaching goes beyond an easy tick-box approach to morality and challenges us at a far deeper level of our being. Few of us have been tempted to make a literal golden calf, even had we the wherewithal and the skills to do so. We are well enough versed in the Judeo-Christian tradition not to bow down before idols of wood and stone, and are daily thankful that Jesus himself is the 'image of the invisible God, the firstborn over all creation' (Colossians 1:15). Had Jesus said, 'You cannot serve God and a golden calf' we could therefore have walked away with our consciences intact. Yet in choosing 'Mammon' or money as God's rival, Jesus has simply not given us that option.

Jesus' words may remind us of Ezekiel's warnings against setting up idols in our hearts (14:4). It may, too, bring echoes of Paul's telling phrase, 'greed, which is idolatry' (Colossians 3:5). For while the golden calf incident was almost inexplicable in its apparently brazen assault on God's revelation at Mount Sinai, it is important that it leads us to a place of humility, not self-righteousness, looking to remove the idols from our hearts before presuming to challenge those in the hearts of our contemporaries or forebears.

A prayer based on Colossians 3:5–17

Lord, today may I put to death whatever belongs to my earthly nature—sexual immorality, greed, rage, malice and dishonesty—and clothe myself instead with compassion, kindness, humility, gentleness and patience. May your peace rule in my heart, and may all that I do and say be done in the name of Jesus, who is my life and my salvation. Amen

GOD IN
THE DESERT

12

SUNDAY: LORD

Now Moses used to take a tent and pitch it outside the camp some distance away, calling it the 'tent of meeting'. Anyone enquiring of the Lord would go to the tent of meeting outside the camp. And whenever Moses went out to the tent, all the people rose and stood at the entrances to their tents, watching Moses until he entered the tent. As Moses went into the tent, the pillar of cloud would come down and stay at the entrance, while the Lord spoke with Moses. Whenever the people saw the pillar of cloud standing at the entrance to the tent, they all stood and worshipped at the entrances to their tents. The Lord would speak to Moses face to face, as one speaks to a friend. Then Moses would return to the camp, but his young aide Joshua son of Nun did not leave the tent.

EXODUS 33:7–11

'And when you pray, do not be like the hypocrites, for they love to pray standing in the synagogues and on the street corners to be seen by others. Truly I tell you, they have received their reward in full. But when you pray, go into your room, close the door and pray to your Father, who is unseen. Then your Father, who sees what is done in secret, will reward you.'

MATTHEW 6:5–6

Among the Bible's varying descriptions of the desert as a place of punishment, of testing and of discipline—and alongside Hosea's tender picture of infant Israel taking her first steps—there is another image in the prophet Hosea that comes as something of a surprise. 'Therefore I am now going to allure [Israel]', says God through the prophet: 'I will lead her into the wilderness and speak tenderly to her... There she will respond as in the days of her youth, as in the day she came up out of Egypt' (2:14–15).

At first sight, the idea of the desert as a honeymoon destination, and so as the perfect place in which to restore a flagging marriage, might seem a little far-fetched. For one thing, the Sinai desert may have sun and sand but it is distinctly lacking in sea and sangria! For another, the impression that the honeymoon itself was a roaring success seems more than a little rose-tinted, especially given the seriousness of Israel's fall, the flagrant act of spiritual adultery in Exodus 32.

Yet, for all its ups and downs, there was something about Israel's wilderness years—especially the period following the golden calf disaster—that proved formative to her understanding of the character of God, the theme of this week's readings. Living in a place of such stark simplicity, between the 'flesh pots' of Egypt (Exodus 16:3, KJV) and the milk-and-honey pots of the promised land, there was little to distract Israel from the task of getting to know God better. Had the honeymoon been more of a success, this would have been the happiest of activities, truly paradise regained. In the event, though, it was against the darkest of backdrops that Israel came to understand more of the 'kindness and sternness of God' (Romans 11:22).

It was the tension between that kindness and sternness that exercised both Moses and God himself in the aftermath of Israel's adultery, and the rest of Exodus 32 sets out that tension in the rawest possible terms. But following the noise and clamour of that chapter, with its sex and violence, the depth of Israel's betrayal and the fierceness of God's anger, it comes as a mighty relief when the narrator finally leads us to Moses' tent—a simple structure (unlike the proposed tabernacle), yet a place where the Lord would speak to Moses 'face to face, as one speaks to a friend'.

As a younger man, Moses had met with God at the burning bush, and it's quite possible that he chose to pitch his tent on the 'holy ground' of that first encounter (Exodus 3). On that occasion, God had not just called Moses but had also revealed a new name to him, 'Yahweh', a word that apparently began as a pun on the Hebrew phrase 'I AM WHO I AM' (3:14). From that moment on, the sacred name Yahweh (or, more accurately, 'YHWH' or 'LORD' in translation) became the standard way in which the Bible writers referred to the God of Israel, with nearly 7000 references liberally scattered through the books of the Old Testament. And as Moses met with this Lord once more in the intimacy of the tent—just as Jesus similarly called his followers to seek out a place of quietness and privacy to do business with their heavenly Father—so Yahweh's servant became Yahweh's friend, just the same progression that we see fleshed out by Jesus in John 15:15.

Exploring the mystery of what 'I AM WHO I AM' really means has absorbed the attention of a thousand Jewish and Christian scholars through the ages. It speaks, of course, of a living God (as opposed to the gods of the pagans who could better be defined by the phrase 'I AM NOT'); and of a Being, too, who is simply incomparable with anything or anyone else (along the lines of Isaiah 40:25: '"To whom will you compare me? Or who is my equal?" says the Holy One'). It bears some resemblance to other mysterious descriptions of God as 'the first and the last' (Isaiah 44:6) and the 'Alpha and the Omega... who is, and who was, and who is to come' (Revelation 1:8); and it may also remind us of the description of Aslan in the Chronicles of Narnia by C.S. Lewis—that he is 'not a tame lion'—since any clearer definition might serve to domesticate him. But perhaps the most illuminating insight emerges from an equally valid translation of the Hebrew: 'I WILL BE WHO I WILL BE'. Moses was given not so much a formula at the burning bush as a reassurance that the God of his ancestors would gradually unfold his true nature through the events that were to follow—not just through acts of sovereign power (as at the parting of the Red Sea) but also through his response to the sheer messiness of Israel's failure and compromise.

That story of Yahweh's faithfulness and Israel's failings is our story, too, as we humbly take our place in God's great history of salvation. Many further chapters of that history have been lived and published: the stories of Joshua and Samuel, of David and the prophets, of Jesus' incarnation, life, death and resurrection, of the Spirit who prompts us to cry out 'Abba, Father', and of the Church that bears his name, each chapter better fleshing out the person of the great I AM in the face of human courage or human fallibility. Yet there is always more to come.

Of two things we can be absolutely sure as we look to the future: first, that Yahweh will always remain faithful to his people; and second, that there will be many surprises along the way. From the burning bush onwards, 'I AM WHO I AM' has never been a tame lion.

A prayer based on Exodus 3

O Lord, the God of our Fathers, the great I AM, I praise you for your kindness and your sternness, for your abundant love and the radiance of your presence. Make me obedient to your call, I pray, and equip me with all I need to play my full part in your great story of salvation. Amen

13

MONDAY: PRESENCE

Moses said to the Lord, 'You have been telling me, "Lead these people," but you have not let me know whom you will send with me... Remember that this nation is your people.' The Lord replied, 'My Presence will go with you, and I will give you rest.' Then Moses said to him, 'If your Presence does not go with us, do not send us up from here. How will anyone know that you are pleased with me and with your people unless you go with us? What else will distinguish me and your people from all the other people on the face of the earth?' And the Lord said to Moses, 'I will do the very thing you have asked, because I am pleased with you and I know you by name.'

EXODUS 33:12–17 (ABRIDGED)

Very early in the morning, while it was still dark, Jesus got up, left the house and went off to a solitary place, where he prayed.

MARK 1:35

Presence is something so basic that we tend to take it for granted until it's removed from us: indeed, the shock of bereavement often centres round this disconcerting fact. When my father-in-law died quite unexpectedly during what had been billed as a routine operation, the feelings of many were expressed by one of my children: 'I just thought Grandad would always be there for us.' It's losing the sense of someone who will 'always be there for us' that is similarly distressing to those abandoned by their marriage partners, whether through adultery, desertion or the strains and stresses of a particularly demanding career.

At the end of the day, as many a remorseful spouse or parent has discovered on returning from yet another trip abroad, even presents are no real substitute for presence.

One of the great themes of the book of Exodus is that of the presence of God, the strongly held conviction that God is there in the midst of his people. Despite receiving the Law on Mount Sinai, the Israelites never defined themselves primarily as the 'people of the book' (a phrase that originates from the Koran rather than from Jewish or Christian sources). Instead they saw themselves as the 'people of the presence'. For 'what else', as Moses put it, 'will distinguish me and your people from all the other people on the face of the earth?'

God's presence had been powerfully experienced on Mount Sinai in the cloud and the fire, but now, as the people prepared to move on, the possibility arose that God might not move with them. It was more a moral and relational question than a geographical one, as aftershocks from the golden calf affair continued to produce serious turbulence between Israel and her Maker. The Lord would continue to be faithful to his promise to Abraham; the 'land flowing with milk and honey' was still Israel's for the taking; but the best God could offer in the immediate aftermath of Israel's fall was an 'angel to go before you' (Exodus 33:2)—better than nothing, but a very poor substitute for God's 'own dear presence to cheer and to guide'.[4]

It was through the repentance of the Israelites (terrified

at the prospect of losing One who had always been there for them), the prayers of Moses and the faithfulness of God that the situation was redeemed, as the Lord moved from 'outside the camp' (33:7) to his former place at the heart of his people. Even then, though, the relationship would take a while to be fully restored. It reminds us, perhaps, of the psalm attributed to a repentant King David: 'Create in me a pure heart, O God, and renew a steadfast spirit within me. Do not cast me from your presence or take your Holy Spirit from me. Restore to me the joy of your salvation and grant me a willing spirit, to sustain me' (Psalm 51:10–12).

As Jesus meditated on Israel's time in the desert, he was deeply aware of his need for God's presence. It was that awareness that led him to withdraw from public ministry early in the mornings, to go to his own secret place where he 'practised the presence of God' (to quote the title of Brother Lawrence's classic text).[5] But this wasn't just practising. As the first Christians in their turn meditated on Jesus, so they realised, quite simply, that he *was* the presence of God— Immanuel, God with us. In the words of a literal translation of John 1:14 (which contrasts neatly with Moses' meeting place 'outside the camp'), 'The Word became flesh and pitched his tent among us.'

'What else will distinguish me and your people from all the other people on the face of the earth?' It's an important question for Christian people and the Church to ask in every age. At times in its history, the Church has been distinguished by its power, wealth and a virtual monopoly on the moral life of a nation. At other times it has been pushed back into the desert, seen as harmless and irrelevant at best, divisive and dangerous at worst. So is the Church (especially in those wilderness years) to be distinguished perhaps by its commitment to high culture or its care of ancient monuments? Is it the Church's involvement in social action that sets it apart, or its contribution to community cohesion, or its all-round decency and niceness?

All of these may have their place, of course. But right at the heart of our Christian distinctiveness lies a calling to be the 'people of the presence of God', daily filled, renewed, strengthened and transformed through Word and Sacrament, and by the power of God's Spirit within. Whatever our aims in life—whatever, too, our sense of failure and compromise—we would do well to emulate the wise example of Moses and regularly repeat his heartfelt words: 'If your Presence does not go with us, do not send us up from here.'

A prayer from the *Veni Creator*, a ninth-century Christian hymn

Come, Holy Ghost, our souls inspire,
And lighten with celestial fire;
Thou the anointing Spirit art,
Who dost thy sevenfold gifts impart. Amen
TRANS. JOHN COSIN (1627)

14

TUESDAY: COVENANT

Moses chiselled out two stone tablets like the first ones and went up Mount Sinai early in the morning, as the Lord had commanded him; and he carried the two stone tablets in his hands. Then the Lord came down in the cloud and stood there with him and proclaimed his name, the Lord. And he passed in front of Moses, proclaiming, 'The Lord, the Lord, the compassionate and gracious God, slow to anger, abounding in love and faithfulness, maintaining love to thousands, and forgiving wickedness, rebellion and sin. Yet he does not leave the guilty unpunished; he punishes the children and their children for the sin of the parents to the third and fourth generation.' Moses bowed to the ground at once and worshipped. 'Lord,' he said, 'if I have found favour in your eyes, then let the Lord go with us. Although this is a stiff-necked people, forgive our wickedness and our sin, and take us as your inheritance.' Then the Lord said, 'I am making a covenant with you.'

EXODUS 34:4–10

Zechariah prophesied, '[God has] shown the mercy promised to our ancestors, and has remembered his holy covenant… that we, being rescued from the hands of our enemies, might serve him without fear, in holiness and righteousness before him all our days.'

LUKE 1:72, 74–75 (NRSV)

Few marriages could survive a flagrant act of adultery committed while on honeymoon, but today's passage marks the beginning of the end of the golden calf affair, with the replacement of the two stone tablets smashed as Moses made his way down the mountain, and a renewal of the covenant between God and his people.

In the previous chapter, Moses had asked to see the Lord's glory, and in today's reading the Lord duly obliged, passing in front of Moses and proclaiming his name in words that would become foundational to Israel's understanding of her God (see, for example, Numbers 14:18; Nehemiah 9:17; Psalm 86:15). So what was at the heart of this unique act of divine self-disclosure? Sternness, yes (for this was not a God to be messed with), but also compassion, grace, forgiveness and patience.

We will focus on the sternness tomorrow and on the apparent injustice of punishing the children for the sins of their parents 'to the third and fourth generation'. But as we look at the seven Hebrew words that express God's generosity and graciousness—adjectives piled on top of another in a lavish celebration of a God who is love—it's all too clear how keenly (almost desperately) the Lord wanted this covenant to work, and how far off the mark is any attempt to portray the vengeful God of the Old Testament as somehow unrelated to the grace-filled God of the New. Indeed, the description of God's character in this passage gives us the only sensible answer to the question, 'Why on earth didn't he wash his hands of the Israelites there and then?'

It is possible to use only impersonal adjectives when we speak of God ('all-seeing, all-knowing, all-powerful') or perhaps to slip into the language of 'first cause', 'life force' or 'the ground of our being'. But the Lord's self-disclosure was deeply personal—intimate, even—moving so far into the territory of human feelings and emotions as to be quite offensive to those who would keep God at a distance.

It is also possible, at the opposite extreme, to attempt to domesticate God, to create a god in our own image— one who bolsters our sense of self-importance, perhaps, as those who are called to be his people. But the Lord's self-disclosure was both loving and fierce, and made at a time when Israel was at her most shameful and undeserving. Grace, compassion, forgiveness and firmness were the hallmarks of this relationship, not some dewy-eyed mutual appreciation society.

However this passage challenges our preconceptions, though, one thing is clear: at a time when choice is king, the idea of covenant—a committed, gracious, lifelong relationship between God and people (or, indeed, husband and wife)—represents a serious challenge to the spirit of the age. The defining image of that age is the supermarket trolley, pushed through acres of aisles and shelving, with an ever-increasing variety of goods on display; and what is true of beer, crisps and dog food is equally true of our values and relationships, our worldviews and the belief systems by which we live our lives. 'I don't want to be tied down' is the language of this approach: 'I want to be free to choose.' Yet all too often we come across the dark side of such unfettered freedom, expressed in unfaithfulness, confusion, addiction, insecurity and an alarmingly toxic environment in which to raise our children and young people.

The covenant between God and Israel involved choice to begin with, of course; and as Zechariah (John the Baptist's father) looked back over the history of his nation, he could only marvel at the 'mercy promised to our ancestors' and at God's continuing commitment to that covenant from Abraham's day to his own. But all other choices on Israel's part (whether those of belief or behaviour) were then to be made in relation to that foundational choice, the commitment to live as the people of God. That might be seen as restrictive and old-fashioned, or, looked at in another way, as protective and secure; for if the 'freedom to choose' were the slogan on one side of the debate, the 'right to life'—a life that is happy, rooted and purposeful—would be a legitimate slogan on the other.

In all this I remember my wedding day, and a small toy dog presented by my best man as he stood up to give his speech. Around the dog's neck was a small medal, and on the medal was the single word 'Fido'. Up till now, said my best man, I'd been free to be a Rover—metaphorically scanning the supermarket shelves for a partner. But from this day on I was called to be a Fido, faithfully committing myself to Bev 'for better for worse, for richer for poorer, in sickness and in health, till death us do part'.

And speaking personally, 25 years on, I'd have to say that Fido, the way of covenant, has proved to be infinitely more fulfilling than Rover, the worship of choice.

A prayer based on Luke 1:68, 78–79

Praise be to you, O Lord, for you have come to us and redeemed us. May your tender mercy shine on all who live in darkness and in the shadow of death, and guide our feet into the path of peace. Amen

15

WEDNESDAY: JEALOUSY

Be careful not to make a treaty with those who live in the land where you are going, or they will be a snare among you. Break down their altars, smash their sacred stones and cut down their Asherah poles. Do not worship any other god, for the Lord, whose name is Jealous, is a jealous God.
EXODUS 34:12–14

When it was almost time for the Jewish Passover, Jesus went up to Jerusalem. In the temple courts he found people selling cattle, sheep and doves, and others sitting at tables exchanging money. So he made a whip out of cords, and drove all from the temple courts, both sheep and cattle; he scattered the coins of the moneychangers and overturned their tables. To those who sold doves he said, 'Get these out of here! Stop turning my Father's house into a market!' His disciples remembered that it is written: 'Zeal for your house will consume me.'
JOHN 2:13–17

The description of jealousy as a 'green-eyed monster' was coined by William Shakespeare, who brilliantly explored the theme in his tragedy *Othello*. If jealousy properly relates to the fear of losing something we already have, and envy to the longing to acquire something that someone else has, then

Iago in the play is consumed with envy and Othello with jealousy. Iago's envy is focused both on Othello's prestige and on the decision to promote a younger man above him. Othello's jealousy is focused, quite unjustly, on the Iago-fuelled rumour that his wife is having an affair.

There is no such thing in the Bible as 'godly envy': in fact, envy regularly finds a place in lists of sinful behaviour (see, for example, Mark 7:22; Romans 1:29; 1 Peter 2:1) and is closely related to the biblical sin of covetousness, itself roundly condemned in the tenth commandment (Exodus 20:17). 'A heart at peace gives life to the body, but envy rots the bones,' warns the author of the book of Proverbs (14:30), while Paul famously writes of love that 'it does not envy, it does not boast, it is not proud' (1 Corinthians 13:4).

While envy belongs pretty clearly in the sin department, though, jealousy (in the sense of a fear of losing something we already have) is a quite different matter. It's true that jealousy can be sinful where it is entirely unjustified or disproportionate (as in the case of Othello). It is equally true that jealousy can be motivated by a sense of humiliation and insecurity more than of love, and can lead to violent and sinful behaviour. But where a committed covenant relationship is genuinely in danger of being destroyed through the unfaithfulness of one of the partners, jealousy is a quite proper response. In the words of the Beloved in the Song of Solomon, 'Place me like a seal over your heart, like a seal on your arm; for love is as strong as death, its jealousy unyielding as the grave. It burns like blazing fire, like a mighty flame' (8:6).

Israel's discovery that Yahweh was a 'jealous God' was rooted in the first and second commandments, 'You shall have no other gods before me' and 'You shall not make for yourself an idol... for I, the Lord your God, am a jealous God' (Exodus 20:3–5, NIV), and the golden calf incident demonstrated that God meant business on this score. Yet this was also a remarkable, even glorious insight, revealing the burning love at the heart of God. Far more deadly in the end would have been some divine shrug of the shoulders, an indifference to the state of this fledgling marriage.

That doesn't fully explain yesterday's reference to the Lord's jealousy extending 'to the third and fourth generation', which at first sight seems unfair as well as contradictory to other parts of the Bible (see, for example, Ezekiel 18, a passage that faces the issue head on). But perhaps the apparent inconsistency focuses on two different understandings of the way the Lord punishes. There is active punishment in Ezekiel ('he is to be put to death', 18:13), while Exodus seems to speak of passive punishment, the natural consequence of a course of action. If a man is unfaithful to his God, and so loses all sense of God's presence and protection, the natural consequence is that his decision will affect the generations yet to come. That's simply the normal pattern, even if Ezekiel would rightly insist that there's nothing fated about such an outcome.

Godly jealousy is extended by Paul to include a pastor's sense of anxiety when his flock are in danger of falling for false teaching (2 Corinthians 11:2), and it can also be applied to the realm of the marriage covenant and to the implicit covenant involved in the bringing up of children. If one child is unjustly favoured above others (as in the case of Joseph in the book of Genesis), there is a quite understandable jealousy on the part of his siblings, who may rightly feel that the parental love due to them is in danger of being lost. Godly jealousy—and specifically a jealousy for the name of God and of his 'house'—also lies at the heart of Jesus' actions in John 2, motivated by the anger that springs from love. The words 'zealous' and 'jealous' don't simply rhyme with one another. At best they share a passion that contrasts markedly with the prevailing apathy and indifference of our day.

The idea that our Lord is a 'jealous God' should therefore act as both an encouragement and a warning to us—an encouragement that, in the words of Isaiah 43:4, 'you are precious and honoured in my sight, and… I love you', and a warning that to spurn this love may spell disaster.

A prayer based on Song of Songs 8:6–7

Praise you, Lord, that many waters cannot quench your love, a love that is stronger than death itself. Place me as a seal on your heart, and help me to abide in you with faithfulness and gratitude, for Jesus' sake. Amen

16

THURSDAY: HOLINESS

The Lord said to Moses, 'Speak to the entire assembly of Israel and say to them: "Be holy because I, the Lord your God, am holy."'
LEVITICUS 19:1–2

'Be perfect, therefore, as your heavenly Father is perfect.'
MATTHEW 5:48

Moses first encountered God on 'holy ground' (Exodus 3:5), and, from that moment on, the word 'holy' occurs well over 100 times before we reach the end of the book of Deuteronomy. In other ancient belief systems, there was no great emphasis on the moral integrity of their gods and goddesses. The Greek, Egyptian and Canaanite deities, for example, were endlessly killing, seducing, manipulating and taking their revenge on one another—'Gods Behaving Badly', to quote the title of a recent novel.[6] Such accounts merely reflected many of the models of human leadership that existed at that time. Only in the religion of Israel did the idea arise of a holy God whose perfect character should be explored and praised and emulated, while the best ethical textbooks of the ancient world (whether those of Plato, Aristotle, Confucius or Marcus Aurelius) were basically humanist documents, making little or no reference to the behaviour of the gods at all.

The frequently repeated motto of the book of Leviticus, 'Be holy because I, the Lord your God, am holy', therefore represents a unique insight into the character of a God who is not simply a fallible human leader writ large. Instead of God reflecting humanity's image (heaven mirroring earth), this insight calls on humanity to reflect God's image (earth mirroring heaven)—an image of glorious perfection and integrity. It's a pattern we see repeated in scripture: we are to be perfect because our heavenly Father is perfect (Matthew 5:48); we are to be loving because God is love (1 John 4:7–12); and, as Christ Jesus 'did not consider equality with God something to be grasped'—we are to be humble as Christ is humble (Philippians 2:5–8, NIV).

At the same time, there is a difficulty with the Leviticus motto. Although we can understand (to some extent, at least) the content of a word like 'love' or 'humility', the content of the word 'holiness' is far harder to pin down. The Old Testament term has a sense of 'otherness' about it, with its root related to the Hebrew word for separation. In fact, virtually everything in the book of Leviticus is divided between the holy and the common, with the common further subdivided into the clean and the unclean. But, along with separation, the word 'holiness' also encompasses God's completeness, his transparency, his moral excellence and the fullness of his character. As the rays of the sun combine all the colours of the spectrum, the holiness of God describes the 'outshining' of all that he is.

How, then, can this dazzling holiness be reflected here on earth? Well, continues Leviticus 19, it can be lived out in the way we respect our mother and father, the poor, the disabled, the foreigner and the elderly. It can be lived out in the loving relationships that should exist among God's people, free from slander, injustice and the desire for revenge. It can be lived out in a commitment to set apart the sabbath and in a steadfast refusal to engage with the occult forces associated with spells, divination and spiritualism. It can be reflected in the way we treat the planet. We will return to some of these themes next week.

It's true that there are also some obscure references in this chapter to clothes 'woven of two kinds of material', to tattoos and to the way we should cut our hair (vv. 19, 27–28). But the sheer down-to-earth practicality and compassion of Leviticus 19 should make it required reading for every Christian believer, particularly those who have long ago written off this particular book of the Bible as irrelevant or worse.

'Be holy because I, the Lord your God, am holy.' There is something deeply attractive about this formulation and its outworking, especially to those who seek a moral life but don't know where to find it. In the New Testament and elsewhere we read of 'God-fearers', Gentiles who were tired of the shenanigans of their pagan gods and the earthly rulers they emulated, and found themselves drawn to the God of Israel instead. They were to be found attached to almost every Jewish synagogue, and some of them were among the very first converts to the Christian faith.

But there is a danger to the formulation too—which is that the positive desire to translate the holiness of God into practical, down-to-earth action can result in the development of a thousand rules and regulations that seek to separate the holy from the common, the clean from the unclean, while leaving the underlying principles of grace and truth in Leviticus 19 far behind. Jesus saw this development among the Pharisees of his day, whose focus on the minutiae of 'holy' living had blinded them to the justice, mercy and faithfulness that lie at the heart of the law. His own life, 'full of grace and truth' (John 1:14), provided the perfect antidote to such a tendency; and perhaps it's because the language of holiness had become debased currency in his day that Jesus chose to rework the old Leviticus motto as he delivered his Sermon on the Mount. Following a passage reminiscent of Leviticus 19 (with their shared concern for positive human relationships), Jesus concluded, 'Be perfect, therefore, as your heavenly Father is perfect.'

Whether we use the language of perfection, holiness, love or humility, the challenge to reflect the God who has called us is quite beyond our reach. The bar has been set very high —impossibly high—and we might conclude that there's no point even attempting to jump it. But that would be a real mistake. For the image here is not of some impossibly demanding taskmaster, driving us towards feats of which we are quite incapable. It is, rather, of a God of transparent holiness (and forgiveness, too), gently drawing us towards himself along the path of compassionate, down-to-earth, Christ-centred obedience.

How wonderful to worship this God, revealed in scripture and through his Son—a God whose holiness acts as both our model and our motivation in pursuing the way of integrity, life and peace.

A prayer based on Isaiah 6:3–8

Holy, holy, holy Lord, my lips are unclean and I stand in need of your purifying presence. As I turn my face to yours, so help me reflect more of your holiness, compassion and truth. Lord, here am I. Send me! Amen

17

FRIDAY: GRACE

You are a people holy to the Lord your God. The Lord your God has chosen you out of all the peoples on the face of the earth to be his people, his treasured possession. The Lord did not set his affection on you and choose you because you were more numerous than other peoples, for you were the fewest of all peoples. But it was because the Lord loved you and kept the oath he swore to your ancestors that he brought you out with a mighty hand and redeemed you from the land of slavery, from the power of Pharaoh king of Egypt.

DEUTERONOMY 7:6–8

'You did not choose me, but I chose you and appointed you so that you might go and bear fruit—fruit that will last.'

JOHN 15:16

It was one of the most humiliating aspects of school life— the selection of two football teams destined to play against one another. First, the teacher supervising the game would choose the captains. Next, the remaining players would line up in a row and would feverishly seek to attract the attention of the captain they most respected. Had orchestras been selected in this way, I would have been one of the first in the line, but football was a quite different matter. Once the real athletes had been snapped up, the two captains would look at the motley crew who remained (of which I would invariably be one) before wearily calling my name.

Today's reading from Deuteronomy metaphorically lines up the nations of the earth and poses the question, 'Why did the team captain—the mighty Yahweh himself—choose Israel to be his "treasured possession"?' On the surface, the Israelites hardly compared favourably with, say, the Egyptians. Numerically, culturally, in almost every way, they were inferior to this brilliant pyramid-building nation and probably to a dozen others who would surely have been eager to attract Yahweh's attention. Yet Israel had not simply been chosen but had been chosen first 'out of all the peoples on the face of the earth'. How could that be? It was simply, we're told, because 'the Lord loved you', just as he'd loved and chosen Abraham, the father of the Jewish nation, many centuries before.

This explanation begs as many questions as it answers, most obviously, 'Did God love the Israelites more than he loved the Egyptians?' But at its heart lie two convictions that remain of the greatest relevance to the Christian believer: first, that God loves us, and second, that such love is undeserved. Put those convictions together, stir them over a low heat and you have the recipe for one of the greatest of all Bible words, the understanding that Yahweh is a God of 'grace'. To have been chosen by this God is no basis for pride or complacency; it is, rather, a cause for astonishment and the deepest gratitude. For the truth is that God's people are frequently the last, not the first, a distinctly motley crew. As Paul put it, 'God chose the foolish things of the world to shame the wise' (1 Corinthians 1:27); and again, 'It is by grace you have been saved… not by works, so that no one can boast' (Ephesians 2:8–9).

There is another answer to the question of why God chose Israel, too: he chose them in order that they might be 'a people holy to the Lord your God'. Part of God's grace to Israel, in other words, was a new sense of mission and purpose—a vocation not simply to bathe in the undeserved love of her Creator but also to live out the qualities of purity and compassion that we were looking at in yesterday's reading. In John 15, Jesus says much the same thing to his disciples: he had chosen them because he loved them (vv. 9–10), but also so that they might 'go and bear fruit—fruit that will last' (v. 16). To find oneself picked by the Captain of captains might seem both surprising and gratifying, but there's a match to be played, not just a glory to be bathed in.

Why did God choose me to be his son or his daughter? It's an important question, and the life of discipleship depends on answering it aright, on steering our way through both the 'not becauses' and the 'becauses' of scripture. We have been saved, writes Paul to his friend Titus, 'not because of righteous things we had done, but because of his mercy', a mercy expressed through the 'washing of rebirth and renewal by the Holy Spirit… so that those who have trusted in God may be careful to devote themselves to doing what is good' (3:5–8). Ignore the 'not because' of these verses and Christians become unattractively complacent and self-righteous; ignore the 'because' and Christians become paralysed with a sense of unworthiness and guilt; but hold the two together—then add that mystery ingredient, the Christian calling to be holy, to bear fruit, to 'devote [ourselves] to doing what is good'—and the full glory of the grace of God is wonderfully revealed. We might even claim that the three things most likely to debilitate people in their Christian pilgrimage—complacency, guilt and a lack of purpose—are each dealt a decisive blow by a true understanding of what God's grace is really all about.

So are the nations still lining up to play in God's team? Will some be chosen and others left behind? That's not the picture we receive from the Old Testament as a whole (see, for example, Psalm 87:4–6 and Amos 9:7), and by the New Testament the answer is explicit: that 'God so loved the world that he gave his one and only Son' (John 3:16), and that 'the Lord... is patient with you, not wanting anyone to perish, but everyone to come to repentance' (2 Peter 3:9).

Perhaps, though, it's the 'new song' of the elders to Jesus the Lamb of God that expresses it best of all:

'You are worthy to take the scroll, and to open its seals,
because you were slain,
and with your blood you purchased for God
members of every tribe and language and people and nation.'
(Revelation 5:9)

A prayer based on John 1:16

Praise you, heavenly Father, that from the fullness of your grace, revealed in Jesus your Son, I have received one blessing after another. Help me to live in your grace, free from both pride and guilt; and may my life today reflect that grace to others, for Jesus' sake. Amen

18

SATURDAY: JUSTICE

Circumcise your hearts, therefore, and do not be stiff-necked any longer. For the Lord your God is God of gods and Lord of lords, the great God, mighty and awesome, who shows no partiality and accepts no bribes. He defends the cause of the fatherless and the widow, and loves the foreigners residing among you, giving them food and clothing.

DEUTERONOMY 10:16–18

'Then the righteous will answer him, "Lord, when did we see you hungry and feed you, or thirsty and give you something to drink? When did we see you a stranger and invite you in, or needing clothes and clothe you? When did we see you ill or in prison and go to visit you?" The King will reply, "Truly I tell you, whatever you did for one of the least of these brothers and sisters of mine, you did for me."'

MATTHEW 25:37–40

It was one of the more unusual episodes of my life: a ten-week trial at the Old Bailey, where I was part of the legal team defending a man against the unique charge of stealing blood from the National Health Service. Four men were eventually convicted of the crime, including an eminent heart surgeon, and duly received prison sentences ranging from six months to three years. But it was salutary to walk beneath Lady Justice every morning—the famous statue that crowns the Old Bailey, complete with sword in one hand and scales in the other—then to witness the balance of the evidence being weighed, a verdict arrived at and the sword of retribution wielded against a most unlikely bunch of criminal conspirators.

A sword and scales is one way to picture justice, and the addition of a blindfold on many depictions of the Roman goddess Justitia helps to convey a sense of impartiality, even if the combination of weapons and blindfolds is hardly to be recommended from a Health and Safety perspective! The picture of justice in Deuteronomy 10, though, is considerably richer than that. It's true that the Lord is defined as one who 'shows no partiality and accepts no bribes'—he is, in that sense, blindfolded—but the way the verse goes on to describe a God who 'defends the cause of the fatherless and the widow' and 'loves the foreigners… giving them food and clothing' is quite revolutionary. We are used to combining the ideas of justice and peace or justice and righteousness, but the link here is between justice and compassion. The hero of this passage is not some cold, impersonal statue but a living Being whose heart burns with love for people, and so with a sense of outrage when those people are bullied, manipulated, abused and mistreated.

The Lord's special love for the 'foreigners residing among you' (or 'resident aliens' in older translations, before the advent of *Close Encounters of the Third Kind* and *ET*) is a theme that we'll return to on a future occasion. It forms an important counterbalance to the parts of Deuteronomy that seem to be advocating genocide, and suggests that the Lord's prime concern was that the promised land should be cleared not of foreign people but of foreign gods. Yet the idea that justice and compassion belong together reaches wider than to resident aliens and helps to explain why human movements for justice can sometimes go so horribly wrong. Without compassion, the call for justice becomes increasingly hard-edged and bitter, violent and oppressive, with the clamour for our rights drowning out all talk of our responsibilities, and yesterday's bullied becoming tomorrow's bullies. As Paul put it in another context, 'If I give all I possess to the poor and surrender my body to the flames, but have not love, I gain nothing' (1 Corinthians 13:3, NIV).

It's perhaps that sense that lies behind the strange instruction to 'circumcise your hearts'—for at its simplest level we clearly need some kind of ongoing heart surgery if even the best things we do are not to be fatally undermined by a lack of godly compassion. From lawyers to politicians, from pastors to community activists, from teachers to doctors, and from philosophers to revolutionaries, there is a tendency (as the years tick by) for a gradual hardening of the spiritual arteries. Even those who start with high ideals and a real desire to make a positive difference are not immune from such a tendency. Increasingly isolated (geographically or emotionally) from those they are seeking to help, ever more aware of the need to insulate themselves from the pain of others, the work goes on but the heart has gone out of it. So what's the answer? Well, says Jesus, it's to put ourselves where the Lord is: to feed the hungry (just as God gives them food in our Deuteronomy reading), to clothe the naked (just as God gives them clothes), to give drink to the thirsty, to welcome the stranger, to visit the sick and bring hope to the prisoner. We need to use our heads as well, of course: there is an ongoing need for strategic thinking and focused campaigning, for discussions and papers and committees and budgets. But it's in direct contact with people (especially poor people) that our hearts will re-engage and godly justice will be matched with godly compassion.

As the second full week of Lent draws to a close, then, what is the picture of God that Israel might have developed over the choppy 'honeymoon period' of her years in the desert? The great 'I AM' defined that picture, the mysterious Lord who could never be tamed or domesticated, a God of white-hot holiness and fierce jealousy, wholeheartedly committed to his people and calling for wholehearted commitment in return. But a God, too, of grace, of justice fuelled by compassion, one whose very presence would remain in the midst of his people, for better for worse, for richer for poorer, in sickness and in health.

'I will never fail you nor forsake you' was the promise of this God (Joshua 1:5), a promise now fulfilled through Jesus his Son, whose parting words to his disciples significantly took the divine name on his lips: 'Surely I am with you always, to the very end of the age' (Matthew 28:20).

A prayer based on Ezekiel 36:25–27

God of justice and compassion, sprinkle your life-giving water on me, that I might be clean; remove from me my heart of stone and replace it with a heart of flesh that beats with your love and fierce compassion; and fill me with your Spirit, that I might live for you as Jesus lived and died for me. Amen

LOVE IN
THE DESERT

19

SUNDAY: GOD

'Hear, O Israel: the Lord our God, the Lord is one. Love the Lord your God with all your heart and with all your soul and with all your strength. These commandments that I give you today are to be upon your hearts. Impress them on your children. Talk about them when you sit at home and when you walk along the road, when you lie down and when you get up. Tie them as symbols on your hands and bind them on your foreheads. Write them on the doorframes of your houses and on your gates.'

DEUTERONOMY 6:4–9

One of [the Pharisees], an expert in the law, tested [Jesus] with this question: 'Teacher, which is the greatest commandment in the Law?' Jesus replied: '"Love the Lord your God with all your heart and with all your soul and with all your mind." This is the first and greatest commandment. And the second is like it: "Love your neighbour as yourself." All the Law and the Prophets hang on these two commandments.'

MATTHEW 22:35–40

'Hear, O Israel': it's the equivalent of a trumpet fanfare or the summons of the town crier, preparing God's people for an announcement of the greatest importance; and the words that follow (the so-called 'Shema' or 'Hear') were to prove so significant to the life of the nation that they continue to be recited daily by practising Jews both morning and evening. They also provide an excellent introduction to our theme this week, as we shift from God's character to Israel's calling, from 'God in the desert' to 'Love in the desert'.

What, then, was this announcement that was to be daily meditated upon, impressed on each succeeding generation and talked about at home, on the road, last thing at night and first thing in the morning? Why was the Shema of such significance that its words were to be tied to the hand and the forehead and written 'on the doorframes of your houses and on your gates'? The first part of the announcement consists of just four words in the Hebrew, 'Yahweh, our God, Yahweh, One', and conveys the fierce monotheism that was to distinguish Israel so clearly from her pagan neighbours. The third part is a renewed challenge to reflect on and obey the Ten Commandments. But it's the middle section—the call to 'Love the Lord your God with all your heart and with all your soul and with all your strength'—that is especially radical and life-changing. Up to this point, the Bible had included summons to obey God, to worship him, to fear him, to bring him gifts, to revere his name. But the Shema was the very first occasion on which Israel was called, quite simply, to love God, and to do so with every part of her being. It's hardly surprising that Jesus later recognised this as 'the first and greatest commandment', the foundation stone of Israel's relationship with her Lord.

Where did the idea of 'loving God' come from? Ancient historians have drawn parallels with international treaties where weaker nations would pledge love and obedience to their overlords in return for security and protection; but these insights, though interesting, don't quite get us to the heart of the matter. It's rather in the family—and especially in the relationship between father and child—that we find the analogy we're looking for, as reflected in the prophets Isaiah, Jeremiah, Hosea and Malachi (1:2; 3:19; 11:1 and 1:6 respectively), and in the book of Deuteronomy itself (1:31; 8:5). The familiar term 'Abba' may well have been coined by Jesus, but the notion of the Father-love of God is well rooted in the Law and the Prophets.

What, then, does it mean to love God today? It's an important question, especially at a time when love is so easily sentimentalised or eroticised, not least in some of the prayers we pray and worship songs we sing. For Jesus (as for the author of Deuteronomy), love and obedience could never be separated—a truth bluntly conveyed in the words, 'If you love me, you will keep my commandments' (John 14:15, NRSV). But if love without obedience is hollow (provoking the response from Jesus, 'Go, and sin no more': John 8:11, KJV), obedience without love is hateful (provoking the response, 'He that is without sin... let him first cast a stone': 8:7, KJV). Love for our Lord—reflecting on his loveliness in our worship and our prayers—is the yeast in the dough, the one ingredient that can guard us from the onset of a stodgy legalism in relation to God, our neighbour, and even ourselves. The desire to please the one we love is at the heart of Shema obedience and remains the only true response to the one who 'first loved us' (1 John 4:19).

In later years, and out of a desire to obey this passage to the letter, faithful Jews wrote the words of the Shema (along with various related texts) on pieces of parchment, then placed them in two small dice-shaped containers known as 'phylacteries' before attaching them to their left hands and their foreheads. Jesus commented on the practice as part of an attack on the hypocrisy of the Pharisees (Matthew 23:5), yet, as a visual aid, it acted as a regular reminder of the demands of the Shema, much as is true of WWJD wristbands today.

Another modern-day phylactery bears a much closer physical resemblance to the two dice-shaped containers of the original; and though I've been unable to trace the origin of the pink fluffy dice that adorn many a car's back window, it might not be too fanciful to suggest some kind of distant link! Yet while the dice speak of life as fun, trivial, superficial, a lottery, the Shema takes us to a place of the deepest seriousness and the deepest joy. Loving the Lord our God with all that we are and all that we have is at the very heart of what it means to be a human being, living in the presence and for the glory of our Creator and Redeemer.

A prayer based on Psalm 116:1–7

I love you, Lord, for you heard my cry for mercy. Because you turned your ear to me, I will call on you as long as I live. Be at rest, O my soul, for the Lord has been good to you. Amen

20

MONDAY: NEIGHBOUR

'Do not hate a fellow Israelite in your heart. Rebuke your neighbour frankly so that you will not share in their guilt. Do not seek revenge or bear a grudge against anyone among your people, but love your neighbour as yourself. I am the Lord.'

LEVITICUS 19:17–18

But [the teacher of the law] wanted to justify himself, so he asked Jesus, 'And who is my neighbour?' In reply Jesus said, 'A man was going down from Jerusalem to Jericho, when he fell into the hands of robbers. They stripped him of his clothes, beat him and went away, leaving him half dead.'

LUKE 10:29–30

It was a good story to be telling in the aftermath of 9/11: the parable of the good Muslim. Two years earlier, I'd been to the summit of Mount Snowdon in the driving rain and had badly pulled a muscle on my way down. Other hikers had walked past, seemingly unmoved by the sight of my increasingly painful progress. Perhaps (who knows?) they included the odd priest or Levite on their way to worship! But the one man to stop was a Pakistani doctor from Bradford who made it his mission to help me down the mountain. Fetching me some painkillers from his backpack and inviting me to lean on him for support, we walked for the best part of a mile together before the painkillers kicked in and I was able to complete the journey on my own. 'Who do you think was a neighbour to the man?' As in the original parable of the good Samaritan, the answer was all too obvious.

If the Israelites were to learn to love the Lord their God in the desert, they were also called to love their neighbours as themselves—though no one prior to Jesus (so far as we know) had ever put these two commandments together as a summary of the Law and the Prophets. Communal life at that point must have had its fair share of stresses and strains, with Jethro's intervention in Exodus 18 suggesting the need for a small army of arbitrators to judge the various complaints and disputes that erupted day in, day out; and without the love that 'covers over a multitude of sins' (1 Peter 4:8), the whole community could all too easily have descended into a seething mass of petty rivalries and resentments.

It's in that context that today's reading (the heart of the so-called 'holiness code' in Leviticus 17—26) became quite so important. We have already looked at the first two verses of this chapter, with their call to 'Be holy, because I, the Lord your God, am holy'; but unless that commandment could be fleshed out in good, honest, loving human relationships it would prove useless—just 'a resounding gong or a clanging cymbal' (1 Corinthians 13:1). Hating a fellow Israelite in your heart, nursing resentments rather than honestly having it out with people, seeking revenge or bearing a grudge: all these were incompatible with the calling to be a holy people. And so to the commandment that sums it all up: 'Love your neighbour as yourself.'

Modern counsellors have frequently made much of the second part of that command, emphasising the need to 'love yourself'; and there can be wisdom in that approach, even if (from a biblical perspective) it places the emphasis in quite the wrong place. Leviticus 19 *assumes* that we love ourselves, much as Paul later does in his letter to the Ephesians: 'After all, people have never hated their own bodies, but they feed and care for them' (5:29). The challenge is rather to 'feed and care for' others, to offer them the same consideration and attention that most of us instinctively give to our own concerns and needs.

In the next few days we will be applying this principle (as Leviticus 19 itself does) to a number of specific scenarios, but Luke's account of the conversation concerning the 'greatest commandment' has the teacher of the law coming back at Jesus with the follow-up question, 'And who is my neighbour?' It's a question to which Leviticus 19 holds an answer, for alongside the provision in today's verses that refers to 'a fellow Israelite', there is another stipulation later in the chapter which clearly (and radically) states, 'The foreigners residing among you must be treated as your native-born. Love them as yourself, for you were foreigners in Egypt' (v. 34). Yet instead of quoting scripture at the man, Jesus famously told him a story that broadens that answer still further, the parable of the good Samaritan.

It's possible that Jesus' story was based on a recent event, in which a Samaritan had gone to a man's aid on the notoriously dangerous desert road from Jericho to Jerusalem. It's possible, too, that it was suggested by an obscure tale from Israel's past, located in the book of 2 Chronicles: during a particularly violent series of skirmishes between Israel and Judah, we read of how the Israelites cared for the prisoners-of-war they had taken, providing them with 'clothes and sandals, food and drink, and healing balm' before setting them on donkeys bound for Jericho, while they themselves headed back to Samaria (28:14–15). Even today, as Tom Wright reminds us, 'few Israelis will travel from Galilee to Jerusalem by the direct route, because it will take them through the West Bank and risk violence.'[7]

Whatever the origins of the story, though, its message is clear: it's the Samaritan, the one who is both close at hand and widely detested, who is included in the remit of the commandment to 'love your neighbour as yourself'. Indeed— and here Jesus deliberately turned the lawyer's question on its head—it is the Samaritan whose compassionate obedience to that very command may one day be needed if you're not going to remain lying in a heap by the roadside.

The call to 'love your neighbour' together with the parable of the good Samaritan (or good Palestinian or Catholic or Jew or Muslim) remain of the utmost relevance in today's world, whether in the context of international diplomacy or against the more personal backdrop of pulled muscles, Bradford doctors, Welsh mountains and the driving rain. Peter once asked the question, 'How many times shall I forgive someone who sins against me? Up to seven times?' (Matthew 18:21). A lawyer once asked the question, 'And who is my neighbour?' And in both cases Jesus' answer took his hearers completely by surprise, pointing to a wideness in God's mercy quite beyond their imaginings.

Love God. Love your neighbour. For any who would seek to separate what God has joined together, we should perhaps give the apostle John the last word: 'If anyone says, "I love God," yet hates his brother, he is a liar. For anyone who does not love his brother, whom he has seen, cannot love God, whom he has not seen' (1 John 4:20).

A prayer based on Ephesians 5:1–2

Lord, enable me to live a life of love today, just as Christ loved me and gave himself up as a fragrant offering. Amen

21

TUESDAY: POOR

'When you reap the harvest of your land, do not reap to the very edges of your field or gather the gleanings of your harvest. Do not go over your vineyard a second time or pick up the grapes that have fallen. Leave them for the poor and the foreigner. I am the Lord your God.'

LEVITICUS 19:9–10

'There was a rich man who was dressed in purple and fine linen and lived in luxury every day. At his gate was laid a beggar named Lazarus, covered with sores and longing to eat what fell from the rich man's table. Even the dogs came and licked his sores.'

LUKE 16:19–21

It was an unusual law by today's standards: a call to deliberate inefficiency. All farmers, then and now, would want to get the very best yield from the land they farmed, especially given the unpredictability of the weather conditions from one year to the next. But as the Israelites prepared for life in the promised land, they were given strict instructions to leave the standing grain at the edges of the fields and not to pick up the gleanings they had accidentally missed. The same applied to grapes and (in a parallel passage in Deuteronomy 24) to olives.

This stipulation was just one of a number of down-to-earth laws designed to protect the poor, whether resident foreigners, widows, orphans or anyone else with no land to call their own. Wages must be paid on time, money must be lent without interest, pledged cloaks must be returned to their owners before sundown and tithes must be offered to 'the Levite, the foreigner, the fatherless and the widow' (Leviticus 19:13; 25:36; Deuteronomy 24:12; 26:12). Meanwhile, the radical provisions of the sabbatical and Jubilee years provided an extraordinary example of wealth redistribution in the ancient world, and one to which we will return in Saturday's reading. 'There should be no poor among you' was the vision held out in the book of Deuteronomy (15:4), although right from the word go it was an aspiration tempered with clear-cut realism: 'There will always be poor people in the land. Therefore I command you to be open-handed toward your brothers and toward the poor and needy in your land' (15:11)

How did Jesus relate to this teaching? One of his distant ancestors, Ruth, who was both a foreigner and a widow, had met her man while gleaning in his fields (Ruth 2), a lovely story that Jesus would have known from his earliest childhood. Meanwhile, the general principle of God's compassion for the poor would have come through Mary his mother, who famously celebrated a God who 'has filled the hungry with good things but has sent the rich away empty' (Luke 1:53). It's true that Jesus shared Deuteronomy's realism on this subject: 'The poor', he once said, 'you will always have with you' (Matthew 26:11). But realism in no way implied indifference. Instead, a number of Jesus' parables spoke to this theme—the story of the rich fool, for example (just the man to harvest to the very edge of his fields), or that of the poor man Lazarus who '[longed] to eat what fell from the rich man's table' (Luke 12:13–21; 16:19–21)—while this 'gleaning' principle might also have been what the Canaanite woman had in mind when she reminded Jesus that 'even the dogs eat the crumbs that fall from their master's table', a response that led to a commendation for her 'great faith' and the healing of her daughter (Matthew 15:21–28).

Elsewhere in the New Testament, the letter of James picks up these themes in such a direct way that some commentators believe that the book started life as a sermon (or series of sermons) on Leviticus 19:12–18.

We should perhaps be careful about using the language of 'positive discrimination' here or of God's 'bias to the poor', especially in the context of the law court: 'Do not pervert justice', counsels Leviticus 19:15; 'do not show partiality to the poor or favouritism to the great, but judge your neighbour fairly.' Yet anyone reading the Bible with a remotely open mind would have to conclude with James that true holiness has two facets: both the negative aspect of '[keeping] oneself from being polluted by the world' and the positive aspect of '[looking] after orphans and widows in their distress' (1:27). It is to the church's great shame that different traditions have often adopted an 'either–or' attitude to these two sides of the holiness coin rather than the 'both–and' approach demanded by scripture.

Returning to the fields with their ragged edges, it is important periodically to celebrate our Judeo-Christian heritage as a nation, not least in the availability of free health care, free education, legal aid and a tax system that massively redistributes wealth from the richest to the poorest. In the last few decades, political parties at both ends of the spectrum have largely avoided all talk of raising taxes (even where the reality has often proved different from the rhetoric). How important, then, for Christians to pay their taxes willingly (in the spirit of Romans 13:6–7) and to extol the virtues of a system that, though flawed, is at least a valid human attempt to encapsulate the biblical vision that 'there should be no poor among you'.

On a more personal level, the gleaning principle speaks both to our wallets and our diaries. To the world outside, the idea of giving a tenth of our income to 'the Levite, the foreigner, the fatherless and the widow' (that is, to the church and to the poor) might seem wasteful in the extreme, every bit as foolish as the deliberate inefficiency of Leviticus 19:9–10. Yet, while people's circumstances differ, the idea of the tithe still seems an excellent target to aim at, as a check on our human greed and an investment in the values of the kingdom of God.

Meanwhile, the constant drive towards efficiency in the workplace—towards proper planning and time management —also seems in danger of squeezing out the generous gleaning principles enshrined in Leviticus 19. Managing our time fruitfully and well is, at heart, a godly activity, and we are right to be concerned about issues of effectiveness and productivity. But where there are no ragged edges in our schedules—no time for listening, for loving, even for apparently 'wasting time' with others (or with God)—there is a real danger that we dehumanise the environment around us, failing even to notice the beggar at our door in our drive to ensure that every grain of wheat is neatly stored away.

Jesus himself had those ragged edges: he steadfastly refused to embrace the urgent schedules that others placed upon him (see, for example, Matthew 9:18–26). How important that we too are generous-hearted enough to respond positively to the interruptions that God sends our way!

A prayer based on James 1:27

Father God, grow within me today a faith that is pure and faultless, with firm foundations when it comes to truth, and ragged edges when it comes to love. Keep me from being polluted from the world and give me your heart for the poor, in the name of Jesus my Saviour. Amen

22

WEDNESDAY: ELDERLY

'Each of you must respect his mother and father, and you must observe my Sabbaths. I am the Lord your God... Stand up in the presence of the aged, show respect for the elderly and revere your God. I am the Lord.'

LEVITICUS 19:3, 32

'For Moses said, "Honour your father and your mother," and, "Anyone who curses his father or mother must be put to death." But you say that if a man says to his father or mother, "Whatever help you might otherwise have received from me is Corban" (that is, a gift devoted to God), then you no longer let him do anything for his father or mother.'

MARK 7:10–12

The call to 'honour your father and mother', enshrined in the Ten Commandments and repeated here in Leviticus 19, is often regarded as 'one for the children'. Many a Sunday school lesson focuses on this theme; many a Christian youth leader addresses it, thus earning the heartfelt appreciation of the parents who dutifully collect their marginally more dutiful offspring at the end of the evening. Caricatures abound of dominating fathers (generally from the Victorian era) demanding respect from their terrified children on the basis of the fifth commandment, while social commentators on juvenile delinquency and the breakdown of manners frequently allude to this teaching, along with the related saying, 'Spare the rod and spoil the child', itself loosely based on Proverbs 13:24.

In Jesus' understanding, though, and at the heart of the original command, the call to honour our father and mother was primarily one for the adults. It was especially as parents approached old age—as they became too frail to work and earn a living—that honouring them became such an important responsibility.

In part, this related to the question of respect: hence the Levitical call to 'stand up in the presence of the aged [and] show respect for the elderly'. There is a dignity in working, in independence and in being financially self-sufficient, with a consequent loss of status when these things become no longer possible. How important, then, that the elderly (whether parents or not) should be properly honoured, both for their past contributions and for their continuing wisdom, care and life experience. Proverbs 23:22 picks up much this same theme ('Listen to your father, who gave you life, and do not despise your mother when she is old'), while the story of Rehoboam, King Solomon's son, who disastrously took the advice of the young hot-heads over that of the wise elders, should act as a cautionary tale, resulting as it did in the collapse of Israel as a united nation (see 1 Kings 12).

Jesus' own relationship with his parents was not straight-forward, though Luke's story of Jesus' visit to the temple as a twelve-year-old boy concludes with the reassuring words, 'Then he went down to Nazareth with them and was obed-ient to them' (Luke 2:51). But it was the behaviour of the Pharisees—in this as in other matters—that increasingly angered Jesus, formed as he was by the Jewish scriptures in general and Leviticus 19 in particular. The Pharisees of his day claimed to be wedded to the Law of Moses, a law that took honouring your father and mother so seriously that the death penalty could be exacted in the most extreme cases of waywardness or abuse. Yet their legal experts had come up with 'Corban', a loophole by which the Pharisees would declare that their property belonged to God alone, thus freeing them from the responsibility of providing financial help for their elderly parents. It was the height of hypocrisy, clothing an act of deep selfishness in the language of sacrifice and piety. No wonder Jesus picked it out as a scandalous example of human traditions overriding the commands of God.

Honouring the elderly, both relationally and (where necessary) financially, remains a high priority for the Christian disciple: indeed, the church should stand out as a place of intergenerational respect, encouragement and learning. The psalmist says of the righteous that they 'will still bear fruit in old age, they will stay fresh and green' (92:14). Paul writes similarly of how 'outwardly we are wasting away, yet inwardly we are being renewed day by day' (2 Corinthians 4:16); and the Christian conviction that death has 'lost its sting' (see 1 Corinthians 15:55) sets the process of ageing in a quite new light, with each new day (whatever its troubles and infirmities) simply drawing us a step closer to the 'eternal glory that far outweighs them all' (2 Corinthians 4:17). It's not that growing older necessarily equates with growing wiser: both virtues and vices can be accentuated as body and mind begin to fail. But the default setting within the Christian community should always be one of the deepest respect towards the elderly: 'Do not rebuke an older man harshly', as Paul puts it to his young protégé Timothy, 'but exhort him as if he were your father' (1 Timothy 5:1).

Are our churches models of 'intergenerational respect, encouragement and learning'? Are they places where the young truly honour the elderly, and the elderly truly encourage the young? Many churches fail that test by unconsciously excluding whole generations of families, young people and children; many others go out of their way to attract these missing generations, but only by alienating their older members or developing some form of age-based apartheid. It is entirely appropriate to develop a range of groups and services for different ages, of course. Yet while we rightly emphasise that children are the church of the present (and not just the church of the future), how important it is to emphasise equally that the elderly are the church of the present (and not just the church of the past).

What of Corban today? It may not exist in the same form as in Jesus' time, but, in the light of contemporary debates about the affordability of long-term care (with assisted dying at the bottom of this particularly slippery slope), we too need to beware of any tendency to find loopholes in our God-given responsibility to honour our elders in general and our parents in particular. Even on the cross—even as he carried the weight of the sin of humanity on his shoulders—Jesus was aware of that responsibility to his mother, placing her in the care of John the beloved disciple now that he himself would be unable to support her (John 19:26–27). How important that we too model a respect for the elderly in word and in action.

A prayer based on Psalm 92:1–2, 14–15

It is good to praise you, O Lord, to proclaim your love in the morning and your faithfulness at night. Keep my faith both fresh and green, I pray, and help me to bear good fruit for your kingdom, for the blessing of those who are old in years and of all whom you love; for Jesus' sake. Amen

23

THURSDAY: SPOUSE

'You shall not commit adultery.'
EXODUS 20:14

'You have heard that it was said, "Do not commit adultery."
But I tell you that anyone who looks at a woman lustfully
has already committed adultery with her in his heart.'
MATTHEW 5:27–28

Today's readings seem to offer a distinctly negative introduction to the theme of love and marriage, and we certainly
have to admit that there is a greater emphasis on 'bad sex' in
the Law of Moses than on 'good sex' (using those phrases
in a moral rather than a physical sense). It's true that we
find the occasional tender reference to 'the wife you love' in
the book of Deuteronomy (for example, 13:6), that young
husbands were exempted from military service for a year to
'bring happiness' to the newly-weds (24:5), and that the
festivals, in particular, provided opportunities for joy and
celebration in the family and beyond (see 16:13–15). But
we need to look elsewhere in the Bible, most famously the
Song of Solomon, for an emphasis on the joy of sex and the
wonder of romantic love.

What is 'bad sex'? The book of Leviticus places a number

of activities in this category, including incest, bestiality, rape, prostitution, and—most controversially in today's climate—some homosexual practices. It was the sin of adultery, though, that uniquely took its place among the Ten Commandments, slotting in at number seven between murder and theft. The commandment was issued to man and woman alike and carried with it the threat of the death penalty for both the partners involved (Leviticus 20:10). In the story of the woman caught in adultery in John 8, it seems that the man got away scot-free, a rather common occurrence in the history of sexual misconduct. But that was never the original intention of a law that drew no moral distinction between adulterer and adulteress.

Mention of John 8 reminds us that we need to read Leviticus through Jesus' eyes—a Jesus who perfectly balanced grace and truth in his response to the woman: 'Neither do I condemn you... Go now and leave your life of sin' (v. 11). As fallen human beings, we have no right to cast the first stone against fellow sinners, and the taking of the moral high ground when it comes to sexual matters is especially arrogant and foolish. That does not mean a soft-pedalling of the Bible's teaching on this subject: Jesus called sin 'sin', and so should we. But it does call for an appropriate humility, a willingness to 'take the plank out of our own eye' before presuming to deal with our wayward brother or sister (see Matthew 7:3).

Talk of planks, though, assumes that sexual impurity is a far more common phenomenon than might be suggested by a straightforward reading of the seventh commandment or the book of Leviticus, and here Jesus' teaching in the Sermon on the Mount is both instructive and challenging. The tenth commandment ('You shall not covet') had already suggested that immoral actions begin in the imagination—in envy, acquisitiveness, maybe sexual desire. Now Jesus took that teaching one step further in his assertion that 'anyone who looks at a woman lustfully has already committed adultery with her in his heart'.

Jesus was not, I think, implying an exact equivalence between lustful thinking and the act of adultery: in the devious minds of fallen human beings, such an equivalence might well lead to the reasoning, 'I've lusted, so I may as well go the whole way!' Instead he was pointing to an inescapable link between the world of our imagination and the world of our actions—a link that is all too frequently denied in discussions on the desensitising effects of pornography and extreme violence. Like the wise doctor who gives forewarning of health problems before they begin to surface; like the wise boss who keeps an eye on future trends even when the company is outwardly thriving, Jesus warns us against an approach that ticks the external boxes while ignoring what's going on inside.

At the heart of this teaching, negative as it may sound, is a glorious vision of love and lifelong faithfulness, along with a holy yet realistic understanding of the wondrous, dangerous gift of sex. It's precisely because human beings thrive in covenant relationships—precisely because men and women need to know that there is someone there for them 'for better, for worse; for richer, for poorer; in sickness and in health, till death us do part'—that marital faithfulness is quite such a prize, and its abandonment quite such a disaster. The progression in Jesus' teaching from eye to heart to hand (a similar sequence to that found in the temptation of Eve in Genesis 3) works equally well as a model for faithful relationships as unfaithful ones; yet one strengthens covenant while the other undermines it. And every wise marriage partner would entirely agree with Jesus' analysis that both trust and betrayal relate to the eye and the heart as much as to the hand and the body.

'May your fountain be blessed, and may you rejoice in the wife of your youth. A loving doe, a graceful deer—may her breasts satisfy you always, may you ever be intoxicated with her love': that is the somewhat heady advice passed on from father to son towards the end of a discourse on the perils of adultery in Proverbs 5:18–19. Appropriately adjusted to cover both sexes, it remains an excellent affirmation of marital love, and one to which all Christian couples should aspire as part of our focus on relationships in this third full week of Lent.

But what of those whose experience is far removed from this picture of marital bliss? Does the world of the desert wanderings have anything positive to say to the single, the divorced, the widowed and the unhappily married? 'Yes' is the answer, and the positive is summarised in the second of Jesus' great commandments, the call to 'love your neighbour as yourself' (Leviticus 19:18). The church is all too often guilty of perpetuating the worst and cruellest of all worlds: holding fast to the Bible's teaching on 'bad sex' while simultaneously ignoring the Bible's equal emphasis on love, warmth, hospitality, vulnerability, community, covenant friendship, appropriate touch, mutual support and a family unit that is bigger than some inward-looking heterosexual pairing. In a highly sexualised culture, where the boundary posts between 'good sex' and 'bad sex' are shifting by the day, the church's first calling is neither to condemn nor to condone but simply to learn how to love.

A prayer based on Psalm 51:1–10

Lord, you know my heart, its hopes and longings, its joys and its secret shames. Create in me a pure heart and a willing spirit to sustain me; and fill me with the riches of your compassion, your mercy and your unfailing love. Amen

24

FRIDAY: REFUGEE

Then the Lord said to Moses: 'Speak to the Israelites and say to them: "When you cross the Jordan into Canaan, select some towns to be your cities of refuge, to which a person who has killed someone accidentally may flee. They will be places of refuge from the avenger, so that a person accused of murder may not die before he stands trial before the assembly. These six towns you give will be your cities of refuge. Give three on this side of the Jordan and three in Canaan as cities of refuge. These six towns will be a place of refuge for Israelites, aliens and any other people living among them, so that anyone who has killed another accidentally can flee there."'

NUMBERS 35:9–15

'You have heard that it was said, "Eye for eye, and tooth for tooth." But I tell you, do not resist an evil person. If anyone slaps you on the right cheek, turn to them the other cheek also. And if anyone wants to sue you and take your shirt, hand over your coat as well. If anyone forces you to go one mile, go with them two miles. Give to the one who asks you, and do not turn away from the one who wants to borrow from you.'

MATTHEW 5:38–42

It's not often that a church community has to deal with the murder of one of its members, but the death of Adam in the late 1980s created massive shockwaves in a church I was shortly to lead. Adam was a young man, a committed Christian, and someone who battled with mental illness. One of his regular practices was to go to the local canal late in the evening, where he would enjoy some solitude and fish into the early hours. It was on one such trip that he was senselessly murdered, a death that was reported later that morning when his body was discovered floating in the canal. His killer was identified soon afterwards and is now serving a life sentence in one of the high-security prisons in London.

Had such an event happened in the ancient world, the consequences would have been clear: the victim's nearest relatives would have had the right to track down the murderer themselves and to kill him. In Israel this practice was allowed on the basis that shed blood 'polluted the land', a powerful image, to which we will return tomorrow. The nearest relative of the deceased would therefore be performing an almost sacred duty by putting the killer to death in obedience to the basic principle of 'life for life, eye for eye, tooth for tooth' (Exodus 21:23–25).

There was even a special name given to the near-relative called to exact this punishment on behalf of his family and clan: the Hebrew word *go-el*. It's a word that is sometimes translated 'avenger' (as in today's reading from the book of Numbers) and sometimes 'redeemer' (as in Ruth 3:9 and Job 19:25). Whatever troubles your closest family members found themselves in—whether poverty, slavery, the confiscation of their lands or even death itself—the *go-el* knew just what was expected of him.

But what if the avenger got the wrong man? Or what if the killing had been accidental, 'without malice aforethought', to use the legal phrase? Someone might fall fatally in the course of a friendly wrestling match; a man might drop a stone from a height without knowing that there was anyone underneath; axe-heads might fly off the handle and kill a neighbour with whom you had set out on a wood-cutting expedition (see Numbers 35:22–23; Deuteronomy 19:5). In such circumstances the family's sense of shock and outrage, together with the pressure on the *go-el* to exact punishment at all costs, meant that the chances of a fair trial were negligible. And here's where the Hebrew idea of asylum came in. Certain Levite towns—six to begin with, spread evenly on both sides of the River Jordan—were to be identified as cities of refuge to which the killer could flee to escape the rough justice of the *go-el*. It's not that reaching one of these towns would automatically save his life: he would later have to stand trial before the community, at which point he would either be freed or sentenced to death. But at least it gave him an all-important breathing space and the chance of a proper and impartial hearing.

The modern concept of a refugee goes far beyond the particular situations outlined in Numbers and Deuteronomy, but there's something about the genuine refugee or asylum seeker—the person fleeing unjust suffering and persecution—that relates very closely to the establishment of the six 'cities of refuge'. Why were those cities all in the hands of the Levites? Presumably because the Levites were the priestly tribe, those committed to a deeper law than the somewhat rough-and-ready law of the clan. The church, similarly, finds itself under a deeper law than the society it inhabits, so giving us both the right and the responsibility to provide sanctuary in the face of unjust or hasty decisions to imprison or deport.

And what of our personal relationships, and the human tendency to bear grudges and take revenge? Well, here Jesus is very clear. It's not that he denies a place for the due process of law in the case of violence and aggression; it's certainly not that he advocates an abuser's charter. But in our normal relationships with those who give us a tough time, our response should be to love and forgive, to turn the other cheek, to give still more than is demanded of us. The cycle of tit-for-tat avenging has no end: it simply escalates, causing ever more tragic devastation in families, communities and nations alike. The only way to break the cycle lies in a determination to stand our ground with dignity but not to retaliate. It's only the prayer of Jesus, 'Father, forgive them, for they do not know what they are doing' that will elicit the centurion's awed response: 'Surely this was a righteous man' (Luke 23:34, 47).

The story of Adam has a surprising postscript. Through a series of events sparked off by his death, his mother came to a living faith in Christ for herself, and later visited Adam's killer in prison. Through her refusal to give way to bitterness and resentment—embracing instead the new life held out to her by her crucified and risen Lord—Adam's death was not so much an end as a beginning. His shed blood may have 'polluted the land' in the terms of Numbers 35:33. Yet, in the famous words of Tertullian (himself responding to a wave of violence against the early Christians), 'the blood of the martyrs is the seed of the church'.

A prayer based on Proverbs 18:10

Lord our Redeemer, your name is a strong tower, a refuge from our accuser and avenger, a place of sanctuary and peace. Free us from bitterness and self-absorption, we pray, that many others might know the safe embrace of your everlasting arms. Amen

25

SATURDAY: LAND

'Follow my decrees and be careful to obey my laws, and you will live safely in the land. Then the land will yield its fruit, and you will eat your fill and live there in safety. You may ask, "What will we eat in the seventh year if we do not plant or harvest our crops?" I will send you such a blessing in the sixth year that the land will yield enough for three years. While you plant during the eighth year, you will eat from the old crop and will continue to eat from it until the harvest of the ninth year comes in. The land must not be sold permanently, because the land is mine and you are but foreigners and my tenants. Throughout the country that you hold as a possession, you must provide for the redemption of the land.'

LEVITICUS 25:18–24

[Jesus] went to Nazareth, where he had been brought up, and on the Sabbath day he went into the synagogue, as was his custom. He stood up to read, and the scroll of the prophet Isaiah was handed to him. Unrolling it, he found the place where it is written: 'The Spirit of the Lord is on me, because he has anointed me to proclaim good news to the poor. He has sent me to proclaim freedom for the prisoners and recovery of sight for the blind, to set the oppressed free, to proclaim the year of the Lord's favour.'

Then he rolled up the scroll, gave it back to the attendant and sat down... He began by saying to them, 'Today this scripture is fulfilled in your hearing.'

LUKE 4:16–21

The rich–poor divide is one of the measures of a civilised (or not-so-civilised) society, and archaeologists have long been able to trace the course of that divide by comparing the size, materials and workmanship of the houses they have excavated. On that measure, early Israel was a reasonably egalitarian society, but the gap widened significantly once there was a king in charge. Perhaps the people should have listened more carefully to the dire health warning issued by the prophet Samuel in 1 Samuel 8: 'This is what the king who will reign over you will do... He will take the best of your fields and vineyards and olive groves and give them to his attendants' (vv. 11, 14).

The secret of Israel's early success on this score lies partly in a series of radical measures that long lay buried in the depths of Leviticus 25—buried, that is, until a group of Christian enthusiasts recognised the relevance of this chapter to the issue of Third World debt, so leading to the creation of the Jubilee 2000 coalition and its later manifestation, the 'Drop the Debt' campaign. We can't know from this distance whether Israel ever fully implemented the programme of Leviticus 25, but the vision behind this chapter is amazing and continues to speak with genuine relevance to modern concerns about poverty and the environment. Indeed, these two issues—poverty and the environment—are inextricably linked in Leviticus, in teaching well ahead of its time.

The connection between the two lies in our relationship with the land: for if the land is fairly distributed and properly

managed, there is every chance that life will become fulfilling, just and sustainable, barring the odd natural or man-
made disaster. In Leviticus 25 the land was to be given
some 'breathing space' every seven years—a fallow period
in which the wildlife had a chance to repopulate itself and
the normal patterns of digging, sowing, pruning and reaping
were replaced by the more nomadic existence of the hunter-
gatherer. Excess crops were to be properly stored every sixth
year, while everyone (from the richest to the poorest) was
to have equal rights to whatever the land produced in years
seven and eight. The whole exercise involved a radical trust
in God the Provider, especially since the system effectively
knocked out not just one but two years of normal food
production.

As if the provisions for this 'sabbatical year' were not
unusual enough, the idea of the 'Sabbath of Sabbaths',
the Jubilee year, was still more extraordinary. At its heart
lay a desire to give everyone a second chance during their
lifetime, an opportunity to escape from the ruin into which
their debt had landed them, a prospect of breaking free
from the humiliation experienced by the homeless and
penniless. Leviticus was clear that Israelites should not be
sold as slaves in such circumstances, but the role of a 'hired
worker' still represented a loss of status and independence.
And so, at the sounding of the trumpet on the Day of
Atonement in the Jubilee year, all debts were cancelled,
all hired workers were freed and all Israelites returned to
their family lands in one massive, instantaneous exercise
in wealth redistribution. This was the 'year of the Lord's
favour' celebrated by the prophet Isaiah (61:1–2). This
was what constituted 'good news to the poor' in a passage
that Jesus took as the text for his first sermon in Nazareth,

famously concluding, 'Today this scripture is fulfilled in your hearing.'

To our ears, the teaching of Leviticus 25 might sound hopelessly naive and idealistic, depending as it does on the Lord to provide bumper harvests every sixth year, and on a pattern of living that cuts right across the normal human character traits of acquisitiveness, workaholism, exploitation and greed. But there's something about godly naivety—about a vision that is simple in its essence but revolutionary in its scope—that can be curiously powerful, effecting real change in a way that more complex, sophisticated approaches often fail to do. The idea that the Jubilee programme could be imposed lock, stock and barrel on contemporary society is quite unrealistic. But the principles behind this chapter— care for the environment, a second chance for the destitute, simplicity, compassion and trust—are every bit as relevant today as they have ever been.

'The land must not be sold permanently, because the land is mine and you are but foreigners and my tenants.' That is the heart of today's teaching, with its echoes in Psalm 24:1 ('The earth is the Lord's, and everything in it!') and in one of Jesus' most pointed parables, where the tenants in a vineyard go on a killing spree rather than giving the landowner his due (Matthew 21:33–41). And while the idea of private ownership is so firmly embedded in our culture as to be virtually unshakeable, the Levitical principles at the very least point us towards a life of fairness and open-handed generosity. In the words of that inspiring little portrait of the Jerusalem church in Acts 4:32, 'All the believers were one in heart and mind. No one claimed that any of their possessions was their own, but they shared everything they had.'

A prayer from 1 Chronicles 29:11, 14

'Yours, Lord, is the greatness and the power and the glory and the majesty and the splendour, for everything in heaven and earth is yours. Everything comes from you, and we have given you only what comes from your hand.' Amen

LESSONS FROM THE DESERT

26

SUNDAY: PROPHECY

The Lord said to Moses: 'Bring me seventy of Israel's elders who are known to you as leaders and officials among the people. Have them come to the tent of meeting, that they may stand there with you. I will come down and speak with you there, and I will take some of the power of the Spirit that is on you and put it on them. They will share the burden of the people with you so that you will not have to carry it alone.' ... However, two men, whose names were Eldad and Medad, had remained in the camp. They were listed among the elders, but did not go out to the tent. Yet the Spirit also rested on them, and they prophesied in the camp. A young man ran and told Moses, 'Eldad and Medad are prophesying in the camp.' Joshua son of Nun, who had been Moses' assistant since youth, spoke up and said, 'Moses, my lord, stop them!' But Moses replied, 'Are you jealous for my sake? I wish that all the Lord's people were prophets and that the Lord would put his Spirit on them!'

NUMBERS 11:16–17, 26–29

'Master,' said John, 'we saw someone driving out demons in your name and we tried to stop him, because he is not one of us.' 'Do not stop him,' Jesus said, 'for whoever is not against you is for you.'

LUKE 9:49–50

After nearly a year of camping by Mount Sinai—a period that extends from Exodus 19 right through to Numbers 10—the Israelites were on the move again; and there's a sense of déjà vu about the middle chapters of Numbers, with pillars of cloud and fire, complaints about food and water, attacks from Amalekites and stories about Moses' sister and father-in-law bringing to mind parallel stories in the middle chapters of Exodus. The Numbers narrative may be a little darker, with an underlying rebelliousness that seems harder than ever for Moses to resolve, but otherwise there's a sense of business returning to normal as the people moved through the inhospitable desert of Et-Tih on their way to Kadesh and the promised land.

It wasn't hunger or thirst but rather the monotonous diet of manna, manna and more manna that provoked the angry complaints in Numbers 11—an incipient riot that started with a group of non-Jewish hangers-on and quickly spread throughout the Israelite community. Moses predictably turned to the Lord in prayer, as he'd done on previous occasions, but this time there was a new edginess to that praying, a sense of anger at God himself for having laid such an impossible weight on Moses' shoulders. 'Did I conceive all these people?' he asked in an outburst remarkable for its feminine imagery: 'Did I give them birth? Why do you tell me to carry them in my arms, as a nurse carries an infant? ... I cannot carry all these people by myself: the burden is too heavy for me. If this is how you are going to treat me, put me to death right now' (vv. 12–15).

For those attuned to Old Testament stories, there are similarities here with the life of Elijah, who similarly moved from a glorious mountain-top experience to a point of near-suicidal depression (1 Kings 18—19). At this stage in their respective journeys, both Moses and Elijah come across as out of their depth, vulnerable and horribly on their own. And in each case the Lord's main response was to deal with that feeling of isolation: to tackle Moses' overwhelming sense of being 'by myself' and Elijah's repeated if misguided complaint, 'I am the only one left.'

In Moses' situation, the approach was aimed at providing the prophet with the personal and spiritual support he needed for the next stage of the journey, no doubt supplementing the administrative support he was already receiving, thanks to his father-in-law's wisdom in Exodus 18. And so, in a dramatic preview of the day of Pentecost, 70 men came out to the tent of meeting to receive the Spirit that was 'on Moses', and, as the full story recounts, proceeded to prophesy 'when the Spirit rested on them' (v. 25).

Two individuals, Eldad and Medad, failed to turn up to the meeting for reasons that are left unexplained. Were they even among those disgruntled characters who were plotting against Moses' leadership, we might wonder? Yet they too received the Spirit and began to prophesy within the camp. And Moses' generous response to Joshua's call to stop them brings to mind Jesus' similar generosity in dealing with unauthorised exorcists and Paul's in confronting unprincipled evangelists (Philippians 1:18). The phrase 'not one of us' employed by the disciples in the exorcism incident clearly needs to be used with extreme caution when it comes to the work of the Spirit, the unpredictable wind of God that 'blows wherever it pleases' (John 3:8).

That same wind (*ruach* in the Hebrew) operated in two ways in Numbers 11, renewing the 70 elders and blowing in a huge flock of quail to supplement the Israelites' dreary rations. But it was not the quails or even the elders that lay at the heart of this incident: it was, rather, Moses' visionary words, 'I wish that all the Lord's people were prophets.' They remind us of the narrative of Luke's Gospel and its sequel in the book of Acts: a story in which Jesus himself appointed 72 others to share in his ministry and in which the Spirit was poured out 'on all flesh', first in a spectacular Jewish Pentecost, then in a lower-key Gentile one (Luke 10:1–17; Acts 2:1–21; 10:44–48). They remind us too of Paul's teaching in 1 Corinthians 14:1: 'Follow the way of love and eagerly desire spiritual gifts, especially the gift of prophecy.'

As we begin the fourth full week of Lent—and as we set off with the Israelites on the second phase of their desert wanderings—today seems an excellent time to pray for a fresh touch of that wind of God, a fresh awareness of his presence with us. And if, like Moses, we are feeling somehow burdened, isolated and out of our depth, perhaps we might pray for that same wind to blow others across our path for mutual encouragement and support. As we've been reminded before, it is not good for man (or woman) to be alone.

A prayer based on 1 Thessalonians 5:16–23

God of peace, today may I rejoice always, pray continually and give thanks in all circumstances. Fill me afresh with your Spirit, I pray, and keep my whole spirit, soul and body blameless at the coming of your Son, our Saviour Jesus Christ. Amen

27

MONDAY: OPPOSITION

Miriam and Aaron began to talk against Moses because of his Cushite wife, for he had married a Cushite. 'Has the Lord spoken only through Moses?' they asked. 'Hasn't he also spoken through us?' And the Lord heard this. (Now Moses was a very humble man, more humble than anyone else on the face of the earth.) At once the Lord said to Moses, Aaron and Miriam, 'Come out to the tent of meeting, all three of you.' So the three of them went out. Then the Lord came down in a pillar of cloud; he stood at the entrance to the tent and summoned Aaron and Miriam. When the two of them stepped forward, he said, 'Listen to my words: When there are prophets of the Lord among you, I reveal myself to them in visions, I speak to them in dreams. But this is not true of my servant Moses; he is faithful in all my house. With him I speak face to face, clearly and not in riddles; he sees the form of the Lord. Why then were you not afraid to speak against my servant Moses?' The anger of the Lord burned against them, and he left them.

NUMBERS 12:1–9

Then Jesus entered a house, and again a crowd gathered, so that he and his disciples were not even able to eat. When his family heard about this, they went to take charge of him, for they said, 'He is out of his mind.'

MARK 3:20–21

Despite Moses' wish that 'all the Lord's people were prophets', there are very few individuals given that specific title in the Pentateuch, the first five books of the Bible. Abraham is portrayed as a prophet during his encounter with Abimelech in Genesis 20, but otherwise it is only the family grouping of Moses, Aaron and Miriam who are described in that way (Exodus 7:1; 15:20; Deuteronomy 34:10). Perhaps it's not surprising, then, that Miriam and Aaron should flex their prophetic muscles in this chapter, in response to what they saw as a serious indiscretion on Moses' part. If anyone was to challenge Moses over his marriage to a Cushite woman, surely they were the ones to do it?

The identity of this mysterious Cushite continues to cause debate among scholars, some identifying her with Zipporah (whom Moses had married many years before: Exodus 2:21) and others assuming her to be a second wife, perhaps a black woman from modern-day Ethiopia. In favour of the first interpretation is a verse in the prophet Habakkuk that parallels Midian (Zipporah's home country) and Cushan (3:7). There is also no suggestion elsewhere in the Pentateuch that Moses had more than one wife.

Whatever the precise details of the situation, though, there is no question that Moses was married to someone outside the Jewish community—and this was at least the stated reason why Miriam and Aaron chose to criticise their brother. Miriam seems to have kept a relatively low profile at Mount Sinai after her inspiring singing and dancing at the parting of the Red Sea. Aaron was only just beginning to regain his prophetic and priestly authority after his role in the golden calf disaster; and the nature of their complaint ('Has the Lord spoken only through Moses? Hasn't he also spoken through us?') suggests that a large dollop of envy may have motivated their opposition to Moses, as much as genuine concerns about his marital status, leadership integrity and spiritual well-being.

We are not given much insight into Moses' feelings at this point—or, indeed, into Jesus' feelings when he was confronted with similar family tensions in Mark 3—but it's not difficult to imagine the anguish inherent in both situations. In Moses' case, the Lord took over, relieving him of the painful task of justifying himself to his siblings; and the various descriptions of Moses in this chapter are among the strongest and most moving affirmations of his character and ministry.

Here was a 'very humble man, more humble than anyone else on the face of the earth'. Here was a man who was 'faithful in all [God's] house'. Here was a man of the deepest visionary insight, someone with whom the Lord spoke 'face to face' (literally 'mouth to mouth'). Miriam and Aaron might well have been prophets, but Moses' prophetic authority was of a quite different order, a uniqueness not based on his leadership status so much as on the quality of his relationship with God. 'He's the best I've got' was the Lord's message to Moses' siblings; and had their brother been able to eavesdrop on the conversation, it might have tested the humility of even the most humble man on the face of the earth!

Interracial marriage is no longer an issue from a Christian perspective, though the wisdom of Christians marrying Christians may be implied in Paul's warning against being 'yoked together with unbelievers' (2 Corinthians 6:14). But Numbers 12, like the chapter that precedes it, reminds us that God is a God of surprises—a God who can pour out his Spirit on Eldad and Medad even when they fail to appear at the appointed rendezvous; a God who can raise up a leader even when his marriage arrangements are not strictly kosher.

It's not, of course, that these stories give leaders a green light to behave exactly as they please: humble Moses would have been the last person to want to be placed on a pedestal. But the reality is that the Lord has to work with who he's got, and both Miriam and Aaron in this chapter and Joshua in Numbers 11 come across as proto-Pharisees, motivated by envy more than grace and focusing on the details while ignoring the bigger picture. 'You strain out a gnat but swallow a camel' is Jesus' summary of this whole approach (Matthew 23:24).

Reflecting on Miriam and Aaron's prophetic inaccuracy on this occasion—and on the confusion among Jesus' family when the eldest son dramatically broke away from the family business and started teaching, healing and casting out demons instead—it's important for us to retain an appropriate openness and humility when it comes to recognising the work of God in his world. It's not that we should politely tolerate gross immorality (or suspected insanity!) among our leaders or blur the distinction between right and wrong. But we should learn the lesson that judgmental arrogance has no place among the children of God. It's that kind of attitude, after all, that could so easily have derailed the ministry of Moses in today's first reading, and that approach, too, that led to the crucifixion of the Son of God.

A prayer based on Hebrews 3:1–6

Thank you, Lord Jesus, that just as Moses was faithful as a servant in all God's house, so you are faithful as a Son over God's house. Help me to recognise wherever your Spirit is at work and to take my proper place within that house, a place of humility, faithfulness, confidence, hope and glory, for your name's sake. Amen

28

TUESDAY: FAITH

The Lord said to Moses, 'Send some men to explore the land of Canaan, which I am giving to the Israelites. From each ancestral tribe send one of its leaders.' So at the Lord's command Moses sent them out from the Desert of Paran... When Moses sent them to explore Canaan, he said, 'Go up through the Negev and on into the hill country. See what the land is like and whether the people who live there are strong or weak, few or many. What kind of land do they live in? Is it good or bad? What kind of towns do they live in? Are they unwalled or fortified? How is the soil? Is it fertile or poor? Are there trees in it or not? Do your best to bring back some of the fruit of the land.' (It was the season for the first ripe grapes.) So they went up and explored the land from the Desert of Zin as far as Rehob, toward Lebo Hamath. They went up through the Negev and came to Hebron... When they reached the Valley of Eshcol, they cut off a branch bearing a single cluster of grapes. Two of them carried it on a pole between them, along with some pomegranates and figs...

They came back to Moses and Aaron and the whole Israelite community at Kadesh in the Desert of Paran. There they reported to them and to the whole assembly and showed them the fruit of the land. They gave Moses this account: 'We went into the land to which you sent us, and it does flow with milk and honey! Here is its fruit. But the people who live there are powerful, and the cities are fortified and very large. We even saw descendants of Anak there.' ... Then Caleb silenced the people before Moses and said, 'We should go up and take possession of the land, for we can certainly do it.'

NUMBERS 13:1–3, 17–23, 26–28, 30

'Do not be afraid, little flock, for your Father has been pleased to give you the kingdom.'

LUKE 12:32

'I spy with my little eye something beginning with "G"': it was a popular game on long car journeys when I was a child, taking its place alongside other well-worn favourites like pub cricket and (as the journey neared its destination) 'first one to spot the sea'. As the exodus drew ever closer to its destination, it was left to twelve tribal elders to become the first to spot the promised land; and as they returned from their comprehensive 40-day exploration, the question of precisely what they had spied was of the greatest possible interest to every Israelite man, woman and child.

So begins a series of events that is told in considerable detail in the book of Numbers, as a watershed in the history of Israel. Here is the culmination of the larger story that first started in Exodus 3 with the burning bush and the call on Moses to lead God's people out of slavery and into a 'a good and spacious land, a land flowing with milk and honey' (v. 8); but it's more than that. Here too is the culmination of a larger story that first began in Genesis 12, the mention of Hebron in today's reading reminding us of God's promise to Abraham at Hebron many centuries before: 'Go, walk through the length and breadth of the land, for I am giving it to you' (Genesis 13:17). But it's more than that as well. Here, finally, is the culmination of the largest story of all, which takes us right back to the garden of Eden in Genesis 1, with the spies' reports of a 'land flowing with milk and honey', of figs and pomegranates, and of a single cluster of grapes that takes two strong men to carry, conveying a vivid sense of 'paradise regained'.

The only trouble with this paradise, though, is that others had got there first. There were two potential answers to the puzzle 'I spy with my little eye something beginning with "G"': one was 'Grapes', the other 'Giants'! It's true that the twelve spies were all agreed that the land was 'flowing with milk and honey': to that extent they recognised that God had kept his word. But while every previous reference to milk and honey had been bound together with God's promise to give the land to his people, the twelve were the first to divide what God had joined together, to split the two words 'promised' and 'land'.

Here, too, is where we see another more personal split emerging, with Caleb (soon to be joined by Joshua) on the one side and the ten remaining elders on the other. We've heard nothing of Caleb before Numbers 13, but from this point on he comes to the fore as a man of faith and courage (see, for example, Numbers 14:24; 32:12; Deuteronomy 1:36; Joshua 14:14). There was certainly nothing half-hearted about his first contribution to the debate (and to the scriptures): 'We should go up and take possession of the land, for we can certainly do it'; and with God on their side, there seemed no good reason why Caleb's counsel should not prevail.

We will take up the story again in tomorrow's readings, but, though Caleb is not mentioned in the New Testament, there is something about his spirit of wholeheartedness that is picked up in Jesus' teaching, especially in Luke 12. Don't worry, Jesus teaches his disciples, about what you shall eat, drink and wear: instead, live a life of radical trust and generosity (vv. 22–34). 'Do not be afraid, little flock, for your Father has been pleased to give you the kingdom.'

Jesus, like Caleb before him, reunites the themes that the spies had sought to divide: the themes of kingdom and gift, of land and promise. He also throws in tender references to the 'little flock' and 'your Father'. It's not that receiving the kingdom of God is an easy matter: for many of Jesus' early followers, it would involve taking up their cross in the most literal of senses, facing the giants of misunderstanding, shame, persecution and even death itself on their way to paradise. But here is where the wholehearted courage of a Caleb was needed—the confidence that 'we can certainly do it'—rather than some timid battening-down of the hatches.

That same courage is urgently needed in the church of today, against the backdrop of declining numbers in many places and growing attempts to marginalise people of faith. The majority report of today's spies, which points to the church's weakness in the face of the giants who surround her, may sound persuasive, but now is a time to 'live by faith, not by sight' (2 Corinthians 5:7) in our mission to bring God's blessing to his world: to reject the way of fear and indecision and to emulate instead the trusting, can-do mentality of a Caleb and a Joshua.

A prayer based on 2 Timothy 1:6–7

Thank you, heavenly Father, for the spirit you have given me: a spirit not of timidity but of power, love and self-discipline. Whatever the giants I face today, help me to fan into flame the gift of faith within me, and to trust in your word and your salvation. Amen

29

WEDNESDAY: FEAR

But the men who had gone up with him said, 'We can't attack those people; they are stronger than we are.' And they spread among the Israelites a bad report about the land they had explored. They said, 'The land we explored devours those living in it. All the people we saw there are of great size. We saw the Nephilim there (the descendants of Anak come from the Nephilim). We seemed like grass-hoppers in our own eyes, and we looked the same to them.' That night all the people of the community raised their voices and wept aloud. All the Israelites grumbled against Moses and Aaron, and the whole assembly said to them, 'If only we had died in Egypt! Or in this desert! Why is the Lord bringing us to this land only to let us fall by the sword? Our wives and children will be taken as plunder. Wouldn't it be better for us to go back to Egypt?' And they said to each other, 'We should choose a leader and go back to Egypt.'

NUMBERS 13:31—14:4

Jesus replied, 'A certain man was preparing a great banquet and invited many guests. At the time of the banquet he sent his servant to tell those who had been invited, "Come, for everything is now ready." But they all alike began to make excuses. The first said, "I have just bought a field, and I

must go and see it. Please excuse me." Another said, "I
have just bought five yoke of oxen, and I'm on my way to
try them out. Please excuse me." Still another said, "I just
got married, so I can't come."'

LUKE 14:16–20

Caleb's rallying call, 'We can do it!' seems to have fallen on
deaf ears, as the remaining spies (Joshua excepted) opted
instead for a 'can't do' mentality. Their initial report had
appeared quite fair to begin with, carefully weighing up the
blessings and obstacles, the grapes and the giants, of their
40-day mission. But in the face of Caleb's wholehearted
confidence, the real feelings of the majority were given full
rein. Indeed, there's something almost surreal about the first
few verses of today's reading, as the residents of Canaan are
transformed into half-human monsters and the promised
land into a death trap.

There are few passages in scripture that more realistic-
ally convey the contagious nature of fear, as the spies first
whipped themselves up into a state of panic, then passed it
on to the people as a whole. In the story of David, we see the
young shepherd-boy confronting his fears in lesser battles
with lions and bears before taking on the mighty Goliath
(1 Samuel 17:34–37); but in Israel's case, those lesser
'battles' had generally proved occasions of abject failure—
think manna, water and golden calves—thus leaving the
people alarmingly vulnerable to the scaremongering of their
appointed representatives.

Moses and Aaron might fall on their faces before the Lord
in holy desperation; Joshua and Caleb might do all they
could to quell the people's terror with renewed talk of a 'land
flowing with milk and honey' and of the weakness of Israel's

enemies in the face of mighty Yahweh (14:5–9). But the sight of God's people fantasising about returning 'home' to Egypt as they stood on the very verge of the promised land is, at the very least, a depressing scene. Indeed, here is the point at which the entire story of the exodus could have seriously unravelled, leaving paradise as lost as ever and the promises to Moses and Abraham shamefully unfulfilled. That was not God's plan—at least, not after the spirited intercession of Moses his prophet—but for a while it looked as though the whole story might end in abject failure.

Jesus' parable of the banquet in Luke 14 could well be read as a commentary on this point of the exodus narrative. In each case, the feast was laid: a 'great banquet' in Jesus' story, mouth-watering grapes, figs and pomegranates in the story of the exodus. In each case, the invitation was issued: 'Come, for everything is now ready'; 'We should go up and take possession of the land, for we can certainly do it.' Yet on both occasions that invitation was spurned, through preoccupation on the one hand and fear on the other. We will look tomorrow at how both stories end. But humankind's reluctance to accept the free gift of God is one of the most challenging of the Bible's reflections on our fallen state, culminating as it does in the story of the one who 'came to that which was his own, but his own did not receive him' (John 1:11).

For today, though, the theme of fear remains highly relevant, given its potential to confuse, to depress, and to force God's people into retreat even on the verge of fresh discoveries and blessings. Yet rather than simply seeking to dispel our fears, as contemporary psychology would have us do, Numbers 14 makes an alternative case for channelling our fears aright—for loving, trusting and fearing God above all else. It's a point picked up in Psalm 34, where the psalmist can say with one breath, 'I sought the Lord, and he answered me; he delivered me from all my fears' (v. 4), and with the next, 'Fear the Lord, you his holy people, for those who fear him lack nothing' (v. 9). It's an insight neatly summarised by Tate and Brady in their metrical version of that psalm: 'Fear him, ye saints, and you will then / have nothing else to fear.'[8] And while we need to be careful in our handling of this theme, there's little doubt that a proper fear of God is the perfect antidote to human panic, enabling us to face the challenges that come our way with a deepening sense of assurance and confidence. 'I spy with my little eye something beginning with "G"' may legitimately lead to the answer 'Giants' or 'Grapes'; but it's only by keeping 'God' in the frame that the grapes will outweigh the giants.

A prayer based on Mark 9:24

Lord, I do believe. Help me to overcome my unbelief. Amen

30

THURSDAY: JUDGMENT

The Lord said to Moses and Aaron: 'How long will this wicked community grumble against me? I have heard the complaints of these grumbling Israelites. So tell them, "As surely as I live, declares the Lord, I will do to you the very things I heard you say: in this desert your bodies will fall— every one of you twenty years old or more who was counted in the census and who has grumbled against me. Not one of you will enter the land I swore with uplifted hand to make your home, except Caleb son of Jephunneh and Joshua son of Nun. As for your children that you said would be taken as plunder, I will bring them in to enjoy the land you have rejected. But you—your bodies will fall in this desert. Your children will be shepherds here for forty years, suffering for your unfaithfulness, until the last of your bodies lies in the wilderness. For forty years—one year for each of the forty days you explored the land—you will suffer for your sins and know what it is like to have me against you." I, the Lord, have spoken, and I will surely do these things to this whole wicked community, which has banded together against me. They will meet their end in this desert; here they will die.'

NUMBERS 14:26–35

'The servant came back and reported this to his master. Then the owner of the house became angry and ordered his servant, "Go out quickly into the streets and alleys of the town and bring in the poor, the crippled, the blind and the lame." "Sir," the servant said, "what you ordered has been done, but there is still room." Then the master told his servant, "Go out to the roads and country lanes and compel them to come in, so that my house will be full. I tell you, not one of those who were invited will get a taste of my banquet."'

LUKE 14:21–24

The widespread panic induced by the majority report of the spies led to the biggest crisis since the golden calf affair, and much of Numbers 14 sees Moses engaging in an activity with which he had become all too familiar over the past year or two: desperate intercession on behalf of a faithless people. In response to Moses' prayerful persistence, the threat of a devastating plague was successfully warded off; but the judgment, when it fell, was still a shattering one. An entire generation of adults (Caleb and Joshua excepted) would fail to make it into the promised land, ironically fulfilling their own ill-fated wish, 'If only we had died… in this wilderness'; while it would be left to the children, the second generation, to fulfil the promises made to Moses and Abraham before him.

Even now, there were some Israelites who wondered if God really meant business. Stung by the harshness of their sentence, they decided that maybe Caleb and Joshua had been right all along and mounted a half-hearted attack on the Canaanites and Amalekites, which was easily repulsed (14:39–45). But perhaps the clearest indication of the Israelites' state of mind at this point is found in a little verse in chapter 16, where poor long-suffering Moses faced yet another plot against his leadership. In a radical distortion of the exodus story, the plotters' charge was as blunt as it was irrational—that Moses was the one who had brought them *out* of a land flowing with milk and honey (Egypt!), only to fail to keep his promises and to kill the Israelites wholesale in the wilderness (v. 13).

There are many echoes of this story in the New Testament, especially in those passages that deal with the call to enter God's kingdom. On several occasions, Jesus described his contemporaries as a 'wicked and adulterous generation' (for example, Matthew 12:39, 16:4), even confronting the self-righteous attitudes of some of that generation with the shocking claim that 'the tax collectors and the prostitutes are entering the kingdom of God ahead of you' (21:32). Meanwhile, Jesus' instruction to his disciples to 'let the little children come to me… for the kingdom of heaven belongs to such as these' (Matthew 19:14) reflects a similar response to the emerging generation as that in Numbers 14, and the parable of the Banquet sees the 'poor, the crippled, the blind and the lame' replacing those more respectable characters who had 'all alike [made] excuses'. 'Brothers and sisters, think of what you were when you were called,' Paul writes to the church in Corinth. 'Not many of you were wise by human standards; not many were influential; not many were of noble birth. But God chose the foolish things of the world to shame the wise; God chose the weak things of the world to shame the strong' (1 Corinthians 1:26–27).

The events of Numbers 13—14 have a sense of inevitability about them for anyone who has followed the Israelites' progress thus far. A steeplechaser who has failed to negotiate various lower hurdles along the course is unlikely to succeed when faced with the final and tallest hurdle of them all. Yet perhaps this observation points to an element of mercy in God's judgment at this point, hard as it might seem— for the generation who had left Egypt had slavery in their bones, with their spirits so crushed and their imaginations so stunted that their ability to 'possess the land' was deeply questionable. It would take a new generation, a generation brought up not as slaves but as herdsmen and shepherds, who would rise to the challenge that lay before them.

As we reflect on this story, and on Jesus' references to children, tax collectors and prostitutes, the 'poor, the crippled, the blind and the lame', there's a lesson here for us. It's so often the unlikeliest of people—those largely unaffected by the comfortable enslavements of wealth, prestige, ambition and achievement—who can show us what it really means to enter into the kingdom of God. That's not to glamorise the life of the poor or to sneer at the best of suburban faithfulness. But it is to recognise that regular contact with those whom the world considers foolish and weak is often the unexpected doorway to life in all its fullness.

A prayer based on Matthew 5:3, 5

Lord, as you promise the kingdom of heaven to those who are poor in spirit; as you promise your inheritance to those who are meek; strip me of my enslaving pride, I pray, and help me to take my place among your pilgrim people on the path that leads to eternal life. Amen

31

FRIDAY: FRUSTRATION

In the first month the whole Israelite community arrived at the Desert of Zin, and they stayed at Kadesh. There Miriam died and was buried. Now there was no water for the community, and the people gathered in opposition to Moses and Aaron. They quarrelled with Moses and said, 'If only we had died when our brothers fell dead before the Lord! ...Why did you bring us up out of Egypt to this terrible place? It has no grain or figs, grapevines and pomegranates. And there is no water to drink!' Moses and Aaron went from the assembly to the entrance to the tent of meeting and fell face down, and the glory of the Lord appeared to them. The Lord said to Moses, 'Take the staff, and you and your brother Aaron gather the assembly together. Speak to that rock before their eyes and it will pour out its water. You will bring water out of the rock for the community so they and their livestock can drink.' So Moses took the staff from the Lord's presence, just as he commanded him. He and Aaron gathered the assembly together in front of the rock and Moses said to them, 'Listen, you rebels, must we bring you water out of this rock?' Then Moses raised his arm and struck the rock twice with his staff. Water gushed out, and the community and their livestock drank. But the Lord said to Moses and Aaron, 'Because you did not trust in me enough to honour me as holy in the sight of the Israelites, you will not bring this community into the land I give them.'

NUMBERS 20:1–3, 5–12

Jesus called [the disciples] together and said, 'You know that the rulers of the Gentiles lord it over them, and their high officials exercise authority over them. Not so with you. Instead, whoever wants to become great among you must be your servant, and whoever wants to be first must be your slave—just as the Son of Man did not come to be served, but to serve, and to give his life as a ransom for many.'

MATTHEW 20:25–28

If Exodus 15 marks the beginning of the first leg of Israel's wanderings in the wilderness (from Egypt to Mount Sinai), and Numbers 10 the beginning of the second leg (from Mount Sinai to Kadesh), Numbers 20 marks the beginning of the third and final phase of the journey, taking the Israelites from Kadesh to the Moabite lands on the east of the River Jordan and within striking distance of the city of Jericho.

Would Moses, along with his sister and brother, make it over the river and into the promised land? Would they be exempted (together with Caleb and Joshua) from the life sentence passed on the rest of their generation, following the Israelites' disastrous fall at the final hurdle? Miriam's death is recorded briefly but significantly right at the beginning of Numbers 20, so it's clear that she was included among those who would 'fall in this desert' (14:32), but how about Aaron and mighty Moses himself?

At first sight, the course of today's passage looks like business as usual, bringing to mind many similar stories involving a perceived need, a grumbling and faithless response, passionate intercession on the part of Moses and the need being finally met, with or without an additional sting in the tail. We've already looked at a near-identical account in Exodus 17, which also culminates in the glorious sight of water gushing out from a rock. It's the end of today's passage, though, that comes as a complete surprise as the Lord almost inexplicably takes the side of the Israelites against Moses and Aaron, reserving the sting in the tail for the two brothers rather than their faithless compatriots. In the past, any betting man would have regarded a punt on Moses as a surefire way to make a pound or two. Yet all of a sudden it seems that Moses' form has deserted him.

What, then, was Moses' misjudgment on this occasion? What sin did he and Aaron commit that proved so significant as to exclude them from the promised land? Along with the Lord's own charge that 'you did not trust in me enough', it's clear that the Israelites here were in real and desperate need—a fact that the Lord himself recognised in commanding Moses to take his staff, gather the community and call forth water out of the rock. For Moses then to address the people as 'you rebels' was quite inappropriate when the Lord himself regarded their request as entirely justified; and for him to continue, 'Must we bring you water out of this rock?' suggests a side to Moses' character—a sarcasm mixed with a nasty whiff of power-play—which is as surprising as it's ungracious. It's true, too, that Moses struck the rock twice rather than obeying the Lord's command simply to speak to it. But his primary sin, at least in the eyes of the psalmist, lay in his 'rash words' more than his disobedient actions (Psalm 106:33).

The images of rock and water are picked up on several

occasions in the New Testament, with Jesus' invitation to 'come to me and drink' (John 7:37) reflected in Paul's meditation on the exodus story in 1 Corinthians 10: 'They drank from the spiritual rock... and that rock was Christ' (v. 4). But perhaps it's Jesus' teaching on leadership that most closely follows the storyline of Numbers 20, with its warnings against the arrogant misuse of power. Moses, we might think, was the last man to be tempted to 'lord it over' others like the 'rulers of the Gentiles'. He was, as we've been reminded, 'a very humble man, more humble than anyone else on the face of the earth' (Numbers 12:3). But today's story demonstrates how no one, not even the humblest, is immune from the frustrations of leadership: to quote 1 Corinthians 10 once more, 'If you think you are standing firm, be careful that you don't fall!' (v. 12).

The danger signals may well have been there for others to see: indeed, here is one of those occasions when Moses might properly have benefited from the further homespun advice of Jethro, his father-in-law and mentor (see Exodus 18). The Israelites had recently received the most devastating of setbacks; Moses had had to weather a series of dangerous leadership challenges as a result; Miriam his sister had just died; and now, to cap it all, the Israelites were grumbling yet again with the same crushing inevitability as in the film, *Groundhog Day*.[9] It's no wonder that Moses snapped.

Yet how important for all God's people—and especially those called to leadership responsibilities within the family, the church, the community and the workplace—to cultivate the gift of self-awareness, most particularly at times of grief, pressure, disappointment and frustration. If even Moses could be turned into a mean-minded little tyrant, it could happen to anyone.

A prayer based on Psalm 139

Lord, you have searched me and you know me. You created my inmost being, and you are familiar with all my ways. Search me, God, and know my heart; test me and know my anxious thoughts. See if there is any offensive way in me, and lead me in the way everlasting. Amen

32

SATURDAY:
ENCOURAGEMENT

Then the Israelites travelled to the plains of Moab and camped along the Jordan across from Jericho... So Balak son of Zippor, who was king of Moab at that time, sent messengers to summon Balaam son of Beor... Balak said: 'A people has come out of Egypt; they cover the face of the land and have settled next to me. Now come and put a curse on these people, because they are too powerful for me. Perhaps then I will be able to defeat them and drive them out of the land. For I know that whoever you bless is blessed, and whoever you curse is cursed.' ... Now when Balaam saw that it pleased the Lord to bless Israel, he did not resort to divination as at other times, but turned his face toward the wilderness. When Balaam looked out and saw Israel encamped tribe by tribe, the Spirit of God came on him and he spoke his message:

'The prophecy of Balaam son of Beor,
the prophecy of one whose eye sees clearly,
the prophecy of one who hears the words of God,
who has knowledge from the Most High,
who sees a vision from the Almighty,
who falls prostrate, and whose eyes are opened:

I see him, but not now;
I behold him, but not near.
A star will come out of Jacob;
a sceptre will rise out of Israel.
He will crush the foreheads of Moab,
the skulls of all the people of Sheth...
A ruler will come out of Jacob
and destroy the survivors of the city.'
NUMBERS 22:1, 4–6; 24:1–3, 15–17, 19

'Blessed are you when people insult you, persecute you and falsely say all kinds of evil against you because of me. Rejoice and be glad, because great is your reward in heaven, for in the same way they persecuted the prophets who were before you.'
MATTHEW 5:11–12

Israel was down but not out. Following Moses' snappy response to the water crisis in the Desert of Zin, and the subsequent death of his brother Aaron recorded at the end of chapter 20, it would be easy to wonder what on earth the future held for God's people and for Moses their leader. Yet just as Israel was truly on the ropes, a measure of relief was offered in the form of a couple of surprise military victories over local warlords Sihon and Og (see Numbers 21:21–35). Meanwhile, a third warlord, King Balak, attempted to employ a weapon of mass destruction against his Israelite opponents—an attempt that was destined to backfire in the most spectacular way imaginable.

The unusual weapon of mass destruction in today's story (and one who, ironically, hailed from modern-day Iraq!) was none other than Balaam, a mercenary pagan prophet who earned a living by issuing curses and blessings at the request of his paymasters. Balaam's name appears in a pagan temple excavated near the Jordan River, where he is credited with preventing a drought through his intercessions, so here was a man well known in the region; and the biblical account of his exploits is genuinely funny, yet with deadly serious intent.

After Balaam had been summoned by Balak, king of Moab, the story of his journey to the Moabite plains includes three encounters with God, the third of which was revealed only through a surreal conversation between the prophet and his donkey. As Gordon Wenham puts it, 'This animal, proverbial for its dullness and obstinacy, is shown to have more insight than the super-prophet from Mesopotamia whom Balak is prepared to hire at enormous expense to curse Israel.'[10] When the prophet eventually arrived, great sacrifices were laid on as a build-up to his solemn act of cursing the Israelites, at which point Balaam proceeded instead to bless them. 'What have you done to me?' asked Balak sorely, to which Balaam piously responded, 'Must I not speak what the Lord puts into my mouth?' (23:11–12).

A second attempt to persuade Balaam to do his worst was equally abortive from Balak's point of view, yet the king persevered, perhaps relying on the adage 'third time lucky'. Once again, great sacrifices were offered; once again, Balaam looked over the Israelites camping in the plain; and once again he found himself unable to curse the people whom the Lord had so clearly blessed. Even Balak's anger couldn't stop Balaam now. Even the thought that he wouldn't get his fee wasn't enough to make him keep his mouth shut (although at least he'd kept his travel expenses to a minimum!). Instead, blessing after blessing fell from Balaam's lips, speaking of Israel's beauty, her special place in God's purposes, the military victories that lay ahead of her and the mysterious 'star' that would come out of Jacob, spelling devastation to the Moabites and those around them. And finally, we're told, 'Balaam got up and returned home, and [a thoroughly disgruntled] Balak went his own way' (24:25).

Jesus never referred to the Balaam story, though the prophet gets some negative coverage elsewhere in the New Testament (see 2 Peter 2:15; Jude 1:11; Revelation 2:14). Yet the idea that the Lord can bring his blessing out of human attempts to curse and persecute his people is one of the great encouragements in the Sermon on the Mount. It's partly that Christians are called to look to the past at such times, 'for in the same way they persecuted the prophets [Moses among them] who were before you'; and it's partly that they are called to look to the future (beyond the Jordan River) 'because great is your reward in heaven'. With such inspiring role models behind us and such a joyful prospect ahead, it's even possible to 'rejoice' at such ham-fisted attempts to destroy the church of Christ.

That's not to encourage a persecution complex, of course, or to confuse the blanket cursing of the church with legitimate criticism. But the Balaam story gives us a rich illustration of a principle first spelt out by Joseph to his brothers and experienced by many generations of believers ever since: 'You intended to harm me, but God intended it for good' (Genesis 50:20).

A prayer based on Hebrews 12:1–3

Lord Jesus Christ, who endured such opposition from sinful people, strengthen and inspire me to run my race with perseverance, fixing my eyes on you and on all that is to come. Amen

BEYOND THE DESERT

33

SUNDAY: HOPE

Remember how the Lord your God led you all the way in the wilderness these forty years, to humble and test you in order to know what was in your heart, whether or not you would keep his commands. He humbled you, causing you to hunger and then feeding you with manna, which neither you nor your ancestors had known, to teach you that people do not live on bread alone but on every word that comes from the mouth of the Lord. Your clothes did not wear out and your feet did not swell during these forty years. Know then in your heart that as a man disciplines his son, so the Lord your God disciplines you. Observe the commands of the Lord your God, walking in obedience to him and revering him. For the Lord your God is bringing you into a good land—a land with streams and pools of water, with springs flowing in the valleys and hills; a land with wheat and barley, vines and fig trees, pomegranates, olive oil and honey; a land where bread will not be scarce and you will lack nothing; a land where the rocks are iron and you can dig copper out of the hills.

DEUTERONOMY 8:2–9

'Then your Father, who sees what is done in secret, will reward you.'

MATTHEW 6:4

The desert wanderings were almost over. The Israelites had camped within striking distance of the promised land. The generation who had escaped from Egypt had all but died out. Moses himself had reached a grand old age, with Joshua, his successor, waiting in the wings. And the book of Deuteronomy takes the form of a final series of sermons from the great man himself, reminding the people of the exodus story, urging them to remain faithful to God and his word, spelling out the glories that await the obedient and the disasters that befall the disobedient, then worshipping the Lord, blessing the people and ascending Mount Nebo to take one final look at the promised land before he died.

As he reflected on the early days of Israel's exodus experience, Moses was entirely honest about what a testing, humbling, difficult time it had proved to be. It's true that the divine name 'Jehovah Jireh' (the Lord who provides) had been completely vindicated. The Lord (as we've seen) had provided daily manna, along with water, protection, vision, leadership, the Sinai law and a host of other benefits. Yet the desert remained the kind of place that either makes or breaks a person, and there had been times when both Israel and Moses himself had come ominously close to breaking point. Had the Israelites indeed 'been home for Christmas',[11] it would have been comparatively easy. But sustaining morale over 40 long years was quite a different matter.

It's important in those morale-sustaining stakes to 'count your blessings, name them one by one',[12] and Moses added two extra blessings to those we have already counted as he preached his long sermon to the people of Israel in Deuteronomy 8. There may have been a continuing need for craftsmen, as a previous reading reminded us, but there seems to have been no need for either tailors or podiatrists:

'Your clothes did not wear out and your feet did not swell during these forty years.'

As Moses continued, though, he moved from the past to the future, powerfully elaborating on what this 'land flowing with milk and honey' was really like. To a people regularly concerned about where their next water was coming from, he emphasised the streams, the pools and the 'springs flowing in the valleys and hills'. To a people bored with the monotony of daily manna, he spoke of wheat and barley, figs and pomegranates, and that greatest prize of all, proper bread! To a people living the most primitive of existences (and perhaps with a nod to the jewellers, the weapon makers and the technologists within his substantial congregation), he concluded with a reference to metals being dug out of the hills. There were dangers ahead as well, as we will see in tomorrow's reading. For now, though, the 'good land' that lay before them was held out as a wonderful future reality, imparting to the Israelites one of the greatest blessings of all, the precious gift of hope.

Jesus didn't elaborate much on the theme of the Christian's promised land in his Sermon on the Mount, though elsewhere he compared the coming kingdom to a banquet, a paradise garden and a house with many rooms (Matthew 22:2–10; Luke 23:43; John 14:2). But right at the heart of his Sermon (and mentioned nine times in just two chapters) was the notion of 'reward', often linked with a commitment to doing our 'acts of righteousness' in secret. 'Reward', for Jesus, was not a mercenary thing: it was, rather, the natural consequence of a particular way of living. As C.S. Lewis helpfully put it: 'Money is not the natural reward of love; that is why we call a man mercenary if he marries a woman for the sake of her money. But marriage is the proper reward for a real lover, and he is not mercenary for desiring it.'[13]

Exactly what the content of 'reward' is within God's future kingdom is a little unclear, perhaps. But the need to emphasise our Christian hope is essential for the morale of God's people, as we, with the Israelites, discover that the Christian journey is more of a marathon than a quick sprint.

How easy it is to lose sight of the truth that 'our light and momentary troubles are achieving for us an eternal glory that far outweighs them all' (2 Corinthians 4:17)! Yet contrary to the old cliché, it's precisely those Christians who are genuinely 'heavenly minded' who will be of real and lasting 'earthly use'.

A prayer based on Jeremiah 29:11–13

Thank you, Lord, that you know the plans you have for me, plans to prosper me, not to harm me, plans to give me hope and a future. In the challenges that today brings, help me to call on you and to seek you with all my heart, for Jesus' sake. Amen

34

MONDAY: PROSPERITY

When you have eaten and are satisfied, praise the Lord your God for the good land he has given you. Be careful that you do not forget the Lord your God, failing to observe his commands, his laws and his decrees that I am giving you this day. Otherwise, when you eat and are satisfied, when you build fine houses and settle down, and when your herds and flocks grow large and your silver and gold increase and all you have is multiplied, then your heart will become proud and you will forget the Lord your God, who brought you out of Egypt, out of the land of slavery... You may say to yourself, 'My power and the strength of my hands have produced this wealth for me.' But remember the Lord your God, for it is he who gives you the ability to produce wealth, and so confirms his covenant, which he swore to your ancestors, as it is today. If you ever forget the Lord your God and follow other gods and worship and bow down to them, I testify against you today that you will surely be destroyed. Like the nations the Lord destroyed before you, so you will be destroyed for not obeying the Lord your God.

DEUTERONOMY 8:10–12, 17–20

[Jesus] told them this parable: 'The ground of a certain rich man yielded an abundant harvest. He thought to himself,

"What shall I do? I have no place to store my crops." Then he said, "This is what I'll do. I will tear down my barns and build bigger ones, and there I will store my surplus grain. And I'll say to myself, 'You have plenty of grain laid up for many years. Take life easy; eat, drink and be merry.'"
LUKE 12:16–19

What was Moses' biggest concern as he continued his sermon in Deuteronomy 8? It was simply this: that the test that lay before God's people was even more challenging than the test that lay behind. Moses wasn't concerned about the existing inhabitants of Canaan, whom the spies had previously described in such alarming and lurid terms (see Numbers 13:31–33). He had no doubt that Joshua would lead the Israelites in a series of successful military campaigns and that Israel would make the land their own. His unease centred rather on the prospect of a prosperous nation, a people 'rich in things and poor in soul'.[14] It's true that the desert had provided more than its fair share of trials and temptations. But it was the promised land that would prove the setting for the biggest temptation of all: the disastrous human tendency to forget the giver in the enjoyment of the gift.

That gift itself was glorious, of course, as we were reminded in yesterday's reading. Never before had this 'good land' been described in quite such rich and mouth-watering detail as the ultimate 'carrot' to compensate for the wilderness 'stick'. But herein lay the danger. The Israelites had already been through 40 years of struggle and deprivation. More struggle lay ahead as they prepared themselves for battle. And the combination of prosperity on the one hand and the sense that they'd worked for it, fought for it—that they deserved it—on the other, is precisely what would lead to trouble. Forgetting the Lord their God, becoming proud, claiming that 'my power and the strength of my hands have produced this for me', regarding their prosperity as a right, maybe even turning to their neighbours' gods—those who would prove less demanding than the Lord himself— these were the temptations that Moses foresaw with a degree of psychological insight that is rich and remarkable. It's no wonder that, alongside the ultimate carrot, Moses warned of a future stick in terms that were both blunt and uncompromising: 'Like the nations the Lord destroyed before you, so you will be destroyed for not obeying the Lord your God.'

It's not difficult to see the relevance of this passage, or of Jesus' parable of the rich fool, for our own time. The tendency to forget the giver in the enjoyment of the gift— indeed, to lose even that enjoyment in the constant lust for more—is a devastating symptom of the foolish condition memorably described by psychologist Oliver James as 'affluenza'.[15] Affluence today has led to far more atheism than poverty ever did. It has also led to an extraordinary plethora of spiritualities that are undemanding and self-centred in their orientation. Deuteronomy 8 is not in any sense world-denying, as the lush descriptions of figs and pomegranates make clear, but the irony of this chapter is well borne out in human experience—that prosperity generally dulls, rather than sharpens, our sense of gratitude and praise. 'Give me neither poverty nor riches', we read in the book of Proverbs, 'but give me only my daily bread. Otherwise I may have too much and disown you and say, "Who is the Lord?" Or I may become poor and steal, and so dishonour the name of my God' (30:8–9).

There are several antidotes to this condition, and we will consider some of them in the next few days. But today's passage offers us a simple choice: a lifestyle based on forgetting the Lord our God on the one hand or remembering him on the other. It is God, we are reminded, who has given humankind 'the ability to produce wealth'. Even the intelligence and hard work that are part of this ability come from him. How important, then, that we remember our gracious Benefactor through our worship, generosity and obedience, and more especially still when times are good—daily practising the presence of God rather than allowing an over-inflated ego to squeeze him out.

A prayer based on Hosea 13:4–6

Lord, thank you for bringing me freedom, for caring for me in the wilderness, for feeding me and meeting all my needs. Thank you that you alone are my Saviour. Keep me from pride, I pray, and a forgetfulness of your presence, that I might live my life today in gratitude and generosity. Amen

35

TUESDAY: FESTIVALS

Celebrate the Festival of Tabernacles for seven days after you have gathered the produce of your threshing floor and your winepress. Be joyful at your Festival—you, your sons and daughters, your male and female servants, and the Levites, the foreigners, the fatherless and the widows who live in your towns. For seven days celebrate the Festival to the Lord your God at the place the Lord will choose. For the Lord your God will bless you in all your harvest and in all the work of your hands, and your joy will be complete. Three times a year all your men must appear before the Lord your God at the place he will choose: at the Festival of Unleavened Bread, the Festival of Weeks and the Festival of Tabernacles. No one should appear before the Lord empty-handed: each of you must bring a gift in proportion to the way the Lord your God has blessed you.

DEUTERONOMY 16:13–17

'"My son," the father said, "you are always with me, and everything I have is yours. But we had to celebrate and be glad, because this brother of yours was dead and is alive again; he was lost and is found."'

LUKE 15:31–32

The three key annual festivals described in Deuteronomy 16 all began life as harvest celebrations. The Festival of Unleavened Bread (which Deuteronomy combines with the Passover, since the two fell at much the same time) took place in the spring as the barley harvest was gathered in. The Festival of Weeks (also known as the Day of First Fruits or Pentecost) took place 50 days later, after the harvesting of the wheat crop. The Festival of Tabernacles (or Succoth, the most important of the three in the life of early Israel) neatly rounded off the agricultural year in the early autumn, with the final threshing of crops and picking of olives, grapes and dates.

Combining God's great (and ongoing) act of creation with his great (and ongoing) work of salvation, the years in the desert imbued these agricultural celebrations with whole new layers of meaning. The Festival of Passover and Unleavened Bread took the Israelites back to the bitterness of their life in Egypt and the glory of their escape to freedom; the Festival of Weeks became a celebration of Israel's rich diet, as compared to the scarcity and monotony of the food in Egypt and the desert; and the Festival of Tabernacles (which included the instruction to construct simple tents from leaves and branches: Leviticus 23:42) reminded God's people of the makeshift dwellings of their desert wanderings. Like the Sabbath, this simple liturgical calendar helped to punctuate the year, a further antidote to the persistent temptations of God-forgetfulness and pride.

What, then, were the features of the three festivals?

First, there was an element of pilgrimage in each, of coming together to a common place (later, of course, the Jerusalem temple): indeed, the Hebrew word for 'festival', *hag*, is closely related to the Arabic *haj*, the Muslim term for the

pilgrimage to Mecca. Next—having gathered together—
there was an emphasis on worship, rest, thanksgiving and
remembrance. There was a generosity and inclusiveness
about the whole enterprise, with gifts presented to the Lord,
and servants, foreigners, the fatherless and widows drawn
into the extended family circle. There was a sense of joy and
celebration, with that lovely phrase in Deuteronomy 16:15
later picked up by Jesus in John 16:24: 'Ask and you will
receive, and your joy will be complete.'

Jesus, of course, took part in the Jewish festivals as a
boy and an adult, with regular references to his Jerusalem
pilgrimages in the Gospel accounts. But it's perhaps in
Luke 15 that the element of community celebration finds
its most moving expression. In place of Passover, Weeks
and Tabernacles, Jesus tells three stories of the lost being
found—a lost sheep, a lost coin and a lost son—and, in
each personal exodus from lostness to foundness, the story
concludes with the calling together of friends and neighbours
in a wonderful release of gratitude and joy.

Since the time of Christ's coming, too, a further layer of
meaning has been added to the old Jewish festivals. Passover
is picked up in the events of Holy Week; the Feast of
Weeks is celebrated as the Day of Pentecost; and the third
Jewish festival—Tabernacles—is more obliquely echoed
at Christmas time, with John's deep reflections on the
incarnation including the famous verse, 'The Word became
flesh and made his dwelling [the Greek word is 'tabernacled'
or 'pitched his tent'] among us' (John 1:14). Christmas,
Easter, Pentecost: the simple agricultural festivals find their
ultimate fulfilment in the person of Christ and the coming
of his Spirit.

If sabbaths and festivals truly punctuate the year, we are

living at a time when such commas and full stops are thin on the ground. In the cities, shops are open 24/7, sweeping away the old distinctions of morning and night, weekday and weekend. Enter those shops and the produce on display will hardly vary from month to month, destroying all sense of 'seedtime and harvest... summer and winter' (Genesis 8:22). The concept of the Bank Holiday lives on as a final vestige of the community festival, and Christmas retains a little of its communal and spiritual power. But, with the ever-increasing detachment from both agriculture and our Judeo-Christian heritage, previously meaningful celebrations have been largely stripped of any wider purpose than a chance for a lie-in, an opportunity for eating and drinking, and a showing of the latest family-friendly movie on the TV.

So does it matter? Is there any real virtue in the idea of holy days, not just holidays, communal sabbaths rather than individual time off, re-creation as compared to recreation? They are good questions, especially given the sometimes dreary nature of the old-fashioned British Sunday. Yet just as good punctuation brings sense and meaning to a piece of prose, so the commas and full stops of sabbaths and festivals bring sense and meaning to our life together. Why has the phrase 'time management' been invented, if it's not from a sense that time itself is out of control? Why do people agonise about their 'work–life balance'? Why the anxiety over 'community cohesion' and the sense of indifference to the foreigners, the fatherless and the widows of today? Could it be that we need to rediscover the meaningful communal celebration, beginning (as we always must) with ourselves, our homes, our families and neighbourhoods?

A prayer based on Psalm 84

Lord Almighty, living God, set my heart on pilgrimage today, that your life in me might make even the desert a place of springs. As the glorious celebration of Easter draws near, lead me to a place of the deepest gratitude and joy: for better is one day in your courts than a thousand elsewhere. To your name be the glory. Amen

36

WEDNESDAY: STORIES

When you have entered the land that the Lord your God is giving you as an inheritance and have taken possession of it and settled in it, take some of the firstfruits of all that you produce from the soil of the land that the Lord your God is giving you and put them in a basket. Then go to the place the Lord your God will choose as a dwelling for his Name and say to the priest in office at the time, 'I declare today to the Lord your God that I have come to the land that the Lord swore to our ancestors to give us.' The priest shall take the basket from your hands and set it down in front of the altar of the Lord your God. Then you shall declare before the Lord your God: 'My father was a wandering Aramean, and he went down into Egypt with a few people and lived there and became a great nation, powerful and numerous. But the Egyptians ill-treated us and made us suffer, subjecting us to harsh labour. Then we cried out to the Lord, the God of our ancestors, and the Lord heard our voice and saw our misery, toil and oppression. So the Lord brought us out of Egypt with a mighty hand and an outstretched arm, with great terror and with signs and wonders. He brought us to this place and gave us this land, a land flowing with milk and honey; and now I bring the firstfruits of the soil that you, Lord, have given me.'

DEUTERONOMY 26:1–10

The man from whom the demons had gone out begged to go with him, but Jesus sent him away, saying, 'Return home and tell how much God has done for you.' So the man went away and told all over the town how much Jesus had done for him.

LUKE 8:38–39

'Lest we forget':[16] it's a phrase that was popularised after World War I, finding its way into the Remembrance Day liturgy and on to gravestones and war memorials up and down the country. Yet when Rudyard Kipling first penned those words, it was not in the context of those lost in war. His concern was rather that the British Empire—in its very prosperity on the eve of Queen Victoria's Diamond Jubilee— might forget that its success was down to God's blessing and not simply to human gifts and talents. 'Lest we forget' echoed the teaching of Deuteronomy 8, in other words, with its warning against God-forgetfulness and pride.

Such teaching was regularly enacted in the three main festivals of Israel's year, as we saw in yesterday's reading, and in the presentation of the first fruits of barley, wheat, olives, grapes and dates that accompanied those events: hence the instruction, 'No one should appear before the Lord empty-handed' (Deuteronomy 16:16). As the offering was made (moving on to today's reading), worshippers were first to recite a simple affirmation that they had 'come to the land the Lord swore to our ancestors to give us', and then to make a longer declaration, spelling out the story of salvation from the days of Jacob (the 'wandering Aramean') to their own. It's as if they were among the 70 who had accompanied Jacob to the land of Egypt many hundreds of years before (Exodus

1:5); among the people of Israel subjected to hard labour as the dream of a new life in Egypt had progressively moved into nightmare territory; among the exodus generation and the generation that followed, who had entered the promised land. This story was not just history. It was rather *their* story, a communal tribute to the work of the Lord in creation and the life of his people.

'My father was a wandering Aramean' has sometimes been described a kind of primitive creed, and it takes its place among the longer liturgical accounts of Israel's early history in the Psalms (especially 78, 105, 106 and 136). In Psalm 78, the purpose of such a creed is made clear: 'we will tell the next generation the praiseworthy deeds of the Lord... so that [they] would know them, even the children yet to be born, and they in turn would tell their children' (vv. 4, 6). There's something about the telling of the story, in other words, that is fundamental to the sense of continuity, of identity, of nationhood. And the very fact that this creed focused on the Lord himself, contrasting his strength with the fragility of his people, instilled in those people a proper patriotism while distancing them from the associated dangers of arrogance and jingoistic pride.

Today's often feverish debate about nationhood and British identity might do well to learn from such an approach, for our increasing reluctance to tell our national story (let alone to do so in the context of the Christian narrative) has led to an alarming vacuum in our national life—precisely the danger that Rudyard Kipling warned against in the words 'Lest we forget'. Into that place have poured forces of extremism, each with competing stories that bear precious little resemblance to truth, let alone to the testimony of a God who is Love;

and meanwhile the social upheavals of the past few decades have contributed to this 'values vacuum', where belief and behaviour alike have increasingly been regarded as purely subjective, personal matters.

Christians are still free to share their individual stories in such a culture—to join the man in today's Gospel passage who 'went away and told all over town how much Jesus had done for him'—and there is often great power in such accounts. But even within the church there is a danger that the wider story of which we're a part remains largely untold, as the Christian creeds are devalued and the scriptures reduced to spiritual pegs on which to hang a variety of personal experiences and opinions. The passing on of this story to 'the next generation... even the children yet to be born' must be done with wisdom, clarity, integrity and attractiveness if it is to make any real impact in the years to come; and the underlying philosophy that promotes the vacuum as the greatest good must be challenged at every point. In the words of a quotation attributed to the Greek philosopher Aristotle, 'Nature [and for that matter, society] abhors a vacuum.'

A prayer based on Ephesians 1, calling us to reflect on our own part in the Christian story

Praise to you, the God and Father of our Lord Jesus Christ, who has blessed us in the heavenly realms with every spiritual blessing in Christ. For you chose us before the creation of the world to be holy and blameless in your sight. In you we have redemption through Christ's blood, the forgiveness of sins, in accordance with the riches of your grace that you lavished on us. With all wisdom and understanding, you made known to us the mystery of your will

according to your good pleasure, which you purposed in Christ—
to bring unity to all things in heaven and on earth under Christ.
Praise to you, O Lord. Amen

37

THURSDAY: CHOICES

Now what I am commanding you today is not too difficult for you or beyond your reach. It is not up in heaven, so that you have to ask, 'Who will ascend into heaven to get it and proclaim it to us so we may obey it?' Nor is it beyond the sea, so that you have to ask, 'Who will cross the sea to get it and proclaim it to us so we may obey it?' No, the word is very near you; it is in your mouth and in your heart so that you may obey it... This day I call the heavens and the earth as witnesses against you that I have set before you life and death, blessings and curses. Now choose life, so that you and your children may live and that you may love the Lord your God, listen to his voice, and hold fast to him. For the Lord is your life, and he will give you many years in the land he swore to give to your fathers, Abraham, Isaac and Jacob.

DEUTERONOMY 30:11–14, 19–20

'Therefore everyone who hears these words of mine and puts them into practice is like a wise man who built his house on the rock. The rain came down, the streams rose, and the winds blew and beat against that house; yet it did not fall, because it had its foundation on the rock. But everyone who hears these words of mine and does not put them into practice is like a foolish man who built his house

on sand. The rain came down, the streams rose, and the winds blew and beat against that house, and it fell with a great crash.'
MATTHEW 7:24–27

At first sight, it was what Americans call a 'no-brainer': a choice between life, blessings and prosperity on the one hand, and death, curses and destruction on the other. The nature of both blessings and curses had been spelt out in graphic detail in the longest chapter in the book of Deuteronomy, chapter 28; and now, as Moses came to the very last words of his very last sermon, he could hardly have put it more clearly or urgently: in the words of the pithiest and most telling of soundbites, 'Now choose life!' Moses' preaching had certainly come a very long way since that day when he had first complained to the Lord, 'I have never been eloquent, neither in the past nor since you have spoken to your servant. I am slow of speech and tongue' (Exodus 4:10).

Was the choice really as simple as that, though? Was it really so obvious that all but the most wilful or stupid of people would automatically make the right decision? What led Eve, then Adam, to taste the forbidden fruit in the garden of Eden, a choice that would surely lead to death, not life? What led the children of Israel to make, then worship, the golden calf? Was it perhaps a sense that the ways of the Lord were simply too perplexing, too burdensome, too demanding; that the sheer cost of life, blessings and prosperity was impossibly high?

To these challenging questions Moses' final sermon gave three strong answers. First, he argued, God was committed to making this thing work, so that even if the worst came to the worst—even if prodigal Israel completely rejected the covenant and ended up in exile—there would always be a warm welcome home (30:1–10). Next, he claimed, God's law was doable, so any idea that it was somehow impossible to follow ('too difficult for you'), mysterious and esoteric ('up in heaven'), or far removed from the problems of everyday living ('beyond the sea') was simply untrue. 'God plays fair' was the message, and his law is understandable, practical, and attainable (vv. 11–14). And finally, Moses asserted, the 'Lord is your life' (v. 20), so any sense of God as a hard taskmaster or a killjoy was ungrateful, misguided and entirely inappropriate.

They were important words as the people of Israel prepared to cross the River Jordan and make the promised land their own. They would be still more important words in later, darker days when first Israel (the northern kingdom), then Judah (the southern kingdom), were carted off into exile by the Assyrians and Babylonians respectively, the national mood swinging between anger at their captors, frustration at themselves and resentment against their God. Indeed, today's passage takes its place among the hope-filled prophecies of Isaiah, Jeremiah and Ezekiel—Jeremiah's proclamation of a 'new covenant', for example, in which the Lord would 'put my law in their minds and write it on their hearts' (31:33) or Ezekiel's resurrection vision of the valley of dry bones (37:1–14).

'The word is very near you'; 'Now choose life'; 'The Lord is your life'. For the Christian believer, these powerful phrases draw us to Jesus, the Word who 'became flesh and made his dwelling among us', the 'way and the truth and the life', the one who promises us life 'to the full' and invites us to 'come to me… for my yoke is easy and my burden is light' (John 1:14; 14:6; 10:10; Matthew 11:28–30). Amazing grace lies at the foundation of this life choice—indeed, there is a wonderful sense in which the truth 'I choose' is constantly reinforced by its reassuring counterpart 'I am chosen' (see John 15:16)—and Moses' command to love the Lord, to listen to his voice and hold fast to him is made far easier now that God has revealed himself in the human face of Christ.

Is the decision to 'choose life' through Jesus—and to do so daily, consistently, through thick and thin—really the no-brainer that it appears to be? Yes and no. As Jesus came to the end of his most famous sermon, he spoke of two builders, two houses, two approaches to life—one embracing discipline, hard work and sacrifice, the other indiscipline, laziness and a cutting of every conceivable corner. In today's context, we might protest that that's not fair, that there are men and women who live life as well as they can, despite struggling to believe the Christian message. But Jesus' primary point is that grace is not cheap: building a house that will withstand the chill winds of discouragement, sickness, even death itself, requires a daily attentiveness to his word and a daily recommitment to embrace the life that is ours in him.

A prayer based on Psalm 95 and Hebrews 3

Living God, today as I hear your voice may I not harden my heart, but rather open it afresh to your truth and love and power. Help me to hold firmly to the confidence I had at first, and to encourage those who are flagging, so that together we might taste the blessings you have promised us in this life and the next. Amen

38

FRIDAY: SUCCESSION

Then Moses went out and spoke these words to all Israel: 'I am now a hundred and twenty years old and I am no longer able to lead you. The Lord has said to me, "You shall not cross the Jordan." The Lord your God himself will cross over ahead of you. He will destroy these nations before you, and you will take possession of their land. Joshua also will cross over ahead of you, as the Lord said. And the Lord will do to them what he did to Sihon and Og, the kings of the Amorites, whom he destroyed along with their land. The Lord will deliver them to you, and you must do to them all that I have commanded you. Be strong and courageous. Do not be afraid or terrified because of them, for the Lord your God goes with you; he will never leave you nor forsake you.' Then Moses summoned Joshua and said to him in the presence of all Israel, 'Be strong and courageous, for you must go with this people into the land that the Lord swore to their ancestors to give them, and you must divide it among them as their inheritance. The Lord himself goes before you and will be with you; he will never leave you nor forsake you. Do not be afraid; do not be discouraged.'

DEUTERONOMY 31:1–8

Then the eleven disciples went to Galilee, to the mountain where Jesus had told them to go. When they saw him, they worshipped him; but some doubted. Then Jesus came to them and said, 'All authority in heaven and on earth has been given to me. Therefore go and make disciples of all nations, baptising them in the name of the Father and of the Son and of the Holy Spirit, and teaching them to obey everything I have commanded you. And surely I am with you always, to the very end of the age.'
MATTHEW 28:16–20

'A hard act to follow': it's a phrase that, in Joshua's mind, could have been tailor-made for Moses as his long life drew to a close. It's true that Joshua had acted as Moses' assistant since the early days of the exodus, that he'd successfully led the Israelite army against the Amalekites, that he (along with fellow spy Caleb) had kept his head while all around were losing theirs,[17] and that he'd had a good few years to get used to the idea that he was next in line for the top job (see Exodus 17:9–14; 24:13; Numbers 14:6; 27:18). But how do you begin to follow a man with whom God speaks 'face to face', a man 'faithful in all my house' and—to cap it all—a 'very humble man, more humble than anyone else on the face of the earth' (Numbers 12:3, 7, 8)?

We will wait till tomorrow for the account of Moses' death, but the answer to Joshua's dilemma—and that of many thousands of leaders similarly called to succeed the godliest and most gifted of predecessors—must start with the conviction that the top job is never up for grabs. As Moses emphasises time and again, 'The Lord your God himself will cross over ahead of you… The Lord will deliver them… The

Lord will do to them... The Lord goes before you'. Knowing that the world is God's world and the church is God's church and the family is God's family—being relieved of the need to carry the ultimate responsibility for everything that happens on our watch—is the greatest of blessings, rooting us in the security that God is in charge and not us. It's a perspective that is equally needed by the leader and the led in times of transition and change: hence Moses' speech, which begins by addressing 'all Israel', then switches to Joshua himself in the presence of the people. It's an insight that demolishes the tendency to regard the best of human leaders as somehow indispensable.

While that ultimate top job is never up for grabs, it remains true that divine leadership is generally 'incarnated', fleshed out in the lives of presidents, pastors and parents alike; and here is where the problems frequently occur as the baton is passed from one leader to the next. Moses, for example, is a man we feel we really know by the time we reach the end of Deuteronomy: we have lived through his highs and lows, his joys and frustrations, his insecurity and tenacity, his whole-hearted wrestling with his God. Joshua, by comparison, is something of a closed book—faithful and courageous, yes, but a man who is easier to respect than to love. Yet Joshua was exactly the person needed for the next stage in Israel's history, a military leader with considerable integrity and strategic ability and one who (in comparison to his predecessor) seems to have had the people of Israel eating out of his hand. We may be squeamish about the task that Joshua was called upon to do, and the violence and bloodshed that would accompany it, but we can't deny that if someone had to do it, Joshua was just the man for the job.

While Moses was a hard act to follow, Jesus, of course,

was the hardest of them all—and the so-called 'great commission' reassured the disciples that this top job was not up for grabs ('all authority in heaven and on earth has been given to me') while also stressing that they still had real work to do ('Therefore go and make disciples of all nations'). The contrasts between today's two readings are as remarkable as their similarities: Moses was addressing many hundreds of thousands of people, Jesus just eleven; Moses was preparing those people for a military task, Jesus for a missionary one; Moses' weapons were the weapons of war, Jesus' weapon the gospel of peace. Yet the call to be 'strong and courageous' and the promise 'He will never leave you nor forsake you' remain just as relevant to the Christian believer as to the Israelites of old.

There are many lessons we could learn from both Moses and Jesus about succession planning and the careful transition from one leader to another. But too great a focus on leadership (whether good, bad or ugly) can easily distract us from the calling on every Christian believer to take up the baton and 'run with perseverance the race marked out for us' (Hebrews 12:1). What is the race marked out for me? What is my place in the purposes of a missionary God? Who will succeed me when my lap draws to a close? These are the questions that today's readings bring into focus, for us all and not just for the favoured few.

Moses, after all, addressed 'all Israel' before summoning Joshua to do his part.

A prayer based on Joshua 1

Lord my God, I thank you that just as you were with Moses, so you are with me—that you will never leave me nor forsake me.

Give me strength and courage for the challenges of today, I pray: place your word in my heart and on my lips, and help me to walk along your path, neither turning to the right nor to the left, for Jesus' sake. Amen

39

SATURDAY: EPITAPH

Then Moses climbed Mount Nebo from the plains of Moab to the top of Pisgah, across from Jericho. There the Lord showed him the whole land... Then the Lord said to him, 'This is the land I promised on oath to Abraham, Isaac and Jacob when I said, "I will give it to your descendants." I have let you see it with your eyes, but you will not cross over into it.' And Moses the servant of the Lord died there in Moab, as the Lord had said. He buried him in Moab, in the valley opposite Beth Peor, but to this day no one knows where his grave is... Since then, no prophet has risen in Israel like Moses, whom the Lord knew face to face, who did all those miraculous signs and wonders the Lord sent him to do in Egypt—to Pharaoh and to all his officials and to his whole land. For no one has ever shown the mighty power or performed the awesome deeds that Moses did in the sight of all Israel.

DEUTERONOMY 34:1, 4–6, 10–12

About eight days after Jesus said this, he took Peter, John and James with him and went up onto a mountain to pray. As he was praying, the appearance of his face changed, and his clothes became as bright as a flash of lightning. Two men, Moses and Elijah, appeared in glorious splendour, talking with Jesus. They spoke about his departure, which he was about to bring to fulfilment at Jerusalem. Peter and his companions were very sleepy, but when they became fully awake, they saw his glory and the two men standing with him. As the men were leaving Jesus, Peter said to him, 'Master, it is good for us to be here. Let us put up three shelters—one for you, one for Moses and one for Elijah.'

LUKE 9:28–33

There's something deeply moving about the sight of Moses climbing a mountain for the very last time—this old man, remarkably fit for his age, ascending Mount Nebo, from which he catches his first and last sight of the promised land stretched out beneath him. These final verses of the Pentateuch take us to the very brink of the fulfilment of the promises made to Abraham way back in Genesis 13: 'Lift up your eyes from where you are and look north and south, east and west. All the land that you see I will give to you and your offspring forever' (vv. 14–15). Yet while Abraham is next commanded to 'walk through the length and breadth of the land' (v. 17), Moses sees it but cannot enter in.

We looked last week at Numbers 20 and at the rashness of Moses' behaviour that led to this prohibition; but it's hard not to feel sympathy for him at the end of the story, as he dies in the land of Moab and is buried in an unmarked grave. Here is a man who spent the early years of his life as an adopted child in the luxury of the Egyptian court; here is a man who forsook all that, spending his middle years as a fugitive and exile in the land of Midian; here is a man who spent his old age in an extraordinary adventure of courage and faith. The last few verses of Deuteronomy are generous in their tribute to Moses as someone who did the impossible—who performed 'awesome deeds' along the way and, more spectacularly still, knew the Lord 'face to face' (when hadn't God himself proclaimed, 'No one can see me and live', Exodus 33:20?). 'Since then, no prophet has risen in Israel like Moses' is the final verdict on a life remarkable for its faithfulness and obedience. But whatever the Lord's own part in the burial, an unmarked grave in the land of Moab still seems a somewhat sad end for such a spiritual giant.

There are two sensible responses to the sense of injustice we may feel on Moses' behalf, and the first is this: that the manner of Moses' death was a fitting conclusion to the life of 'a very humble man, more humble than anyone else on the face of the earth' (Numbers 12:3). Given the Israelites' later propensity for worshipping at shrines dedicated to other gods, there was even a danger that Moses' resting place might become a stumbling block for them, the focus of a veneration bordering on the idolatrous—and nothing could have been further from the understanding or the wishes of Moses himself.

The second response is more intriguing still, for there is strong evidence that the book of Deuteronomy was edited into its final form long after Moses' death, perhaps in the days around the Babylonian exile. This was the time when the prophet Isaiah was beginning to speak of the mysterious 'suffering servant', one who would face injustice, pain and death on behalf of God's people before seeing the 'light of life' once more (see Isaiah 53). Could it be that humble Moses, memorably described in today's reading as 'the servant of the Lord', was a forerunner of Isaiah's suffering servant, a precursor ultimately of Jesus Christ himself?

It's that thought that gives additional significance to the visionary encounter between Moses, Elijah and Jesus on the mount of transfiguration, where (as we have already seen) the

Greek term in the phrase 'they spoke about his departure' is the word *exodos*. Moses, of course, was supremely qualified to speak on the theme of exodus. As Jesus faced up to the terrifying ordeal of the first Holy Week, Moses' presence could only have been an encouragement and an inspiration. Yet, while Moses' exodus was ultimately incomplete ('a shadow', as the writer to the Hebrews put it, 'of the good things that are coming': 10:1), Jesus' exodus would be '[brought to] fulfilment at Jerusalem', the place of death and resurrection through which 'many sons and daughters' would be brought to glory (see Hebrews 2:10).

We are now on the eve of Holy Week, the conclusion of our walk in the desert, and over the coming days we will look at various images from the 'shadow'—from Israel's exodus—which help to explain the 'good things' at the heart of Jesus' journey to death and beyond. But as we come to the end of the story of Moses himself, some further words from the letter to the Hebrews come to mind, words that apply to all the Old Testament heroes of faith, Abraham and Moses pre-eminent among them:

All these people were still living by faith when they died. They did not receive the things promised; they only saw them and welcomed them from a distance, admitting that they were foreigners and strangers on earth... If they had been thinking of the country they had left, they would have had opportunity to return. Instead, they were longing for a better country—a heavenly one. Therefore God is not ashamed to be called their God, for he has prepared a city for them. (11:13, 15–16)

A prayer based on Psalm 103

I praise you, Lord, that your ways were made known to Moses, and your deeds to the people of Israel. I praise you for your message of justice and compassion, of healing and forgiveness, for the wonder of your covenant love for your people. From everlasting to everlasting you are my God and I am your child. Praise the Lord, O my soul, and forget not all his benefits. Amen

THE CROSS
IN THE DESERT

40

PALM SUNDAY: KING

When you enter the land the Lord your God is giving you and have taken possession of it and settled in it, and you say, 'Let us set a king over us like all the nations around us,' be sure to appoint over you the king the Lord your God chooses. He must be from among your own people. Do not place a foreigner over you, one who is not an Israelite. The king, moreover, must not acquire great numbers of horses for himself or make the people return to Egypt to get more of them, for the Lord has told you, 'You are not to go back that way again.' He must not take many wives, or his heart will be led astray. He must not accumulate large amounts of silver and gold. When he takes the throne of his kingdom, he is to write for himself on a scroll a copy of this law, taken from that of the Levitical priests. It is to be with him, and he is to read it all the days of his life so that he may learn to revere the Lord his God and follow carefully all the words of this law and these decrees and not consider himself better than his fellow Israelites and turn from the law to the right or to the left. Then he and his descendants will reign a long time over his kingdom in Israel.

DEUTERONOMY 17:14–20

The next day the great crowd that had come for the Feast heard that Jesus was on his way to Jerusalem. They took palm branches and went out to meet him, shouting, 'Hosanna!' 'Blessed is he who comes in the name of the Lord!' 'Blessed is the King of Israel!' Jesus found a young donkey and sat upon it, as it is written: 'Do not be afraid, O Daughter of Zion; see, your king is coming, seated on a donkey's colt.'
JOHN 12:12–15

Money, Sex and Power: it's the title of a helpful book by Richard Foster,[18] relating the monastic vows of poverty, chastity and obedience to our own day. Yet long before Richard Foster wrote his book, and even before the newly emerging religious communities penned their Rules of Life a thousand years earlier, the delights and dangers of money, sex and power were well recognised, not least in the Old Testament scriptures themselves.

Although its precise background is disputed, there's no doubt that Deuteronomy 17 is one of the most ancient and important Jewish reflections on the nature of kingship, and its principles remain immensely relevant today. On money we read, '[The king] must not accumulate large amounts of silver and gold'; on sex, 'He must not take many wives, or his heart will be led astray'; on power, '[He] must not acquire great numbers of horses for himself or make the people return to Egypt to get more of them.' Of course, these three temptations were all interlinked, for what better way to establish powerful political alliances than through marriages (and as many of them as possible)? What better way to protect wealth than through multiplying horses, building a formidable cavalry, even engaging in arms trading with their old foes, the Egyptians?

Power tends to corrupt, though, and often in the most gradual and subtle of ways; and here is where Moses recognised that action was needed alongside his words of warning. The selection of the king was part of that action (a matter of prophetic discernment above all else): 'Be sure to appoint over you the king the Lord your God chooses.' Yet once selected, the candidate was to undertake a solemn and enduring discipline: writing his own copy of the book of the law, then reading it and meditating on it all the days of his life.

The king, in other words, was to be a man *under* authority before he could ever be a man *in* authority; and if the heart of the Law was indeed to 'love the Lord your God' and to 'love your neighbour as yourself', this daily discipline would enable him to 'revere the Lord' as well as protecting him from that most insidious of temptations—the alarming tendency to 'consider himself better than his fellow Israelites'.

As King Jesus made his way into Jerusalem, the excited adulation of the crowd ringing in his ears, it's astonishing to read how completely and radically he embraced Deuteronomy's model of kingship. All thought of 'great numbers of horses'—of some impressive military manoeuvre against the forces of Rome—was completely subverted by the sight of a man on a donkey (and not a very big donkey, at that). Any idea of grubby political alliances, of palaces and harems, of wealth and weaponry was similarly swept aside. Here was a man 'from among your own people' who would shortly be washing the feet of his disciples, 'not consider[ing] himself better than his fellow Israelites'. Here was a man under authority, the perfect fulfilment of that great prophecy in the book of Jeremiah, 'I will put my law in their minds and write it on their hearts' (31:33).

And despite the trappings—despite the lowly hatchback, not the lavish limousine—here was a man worthy of the most extravagant expressions of celebration and praise.

As we join in the praise of those crowds on the first Palm Sunday—as we join, too, in the worship of the angels and the archangels at the glorious vision of Jesus, our servant king—there is much to reflect on today. At a time of great suspicion towards those in authority, in a culture whose default position is to assume that people are 'only in it for what they can get out of it', it's especially important to acknowledge the seductive nature of power and to pick up on any early symptoms of that seduction in ourselves or others. We can legislate against the misuse of power, of course. We can cherish media that are free to investigate, to challenge and to criticise (provided, as with our trading system, that the concept of free speech is properly balanced by the concept of fair speech). But while our focus is purely on prevention, on prohibition, on threat, we are only doing half the job.

The reality is that the temptations relating to money, sex and power will never be tackled if we face them head on. The only antidote, as both Moses and Jesus recognised, is a daily discipline of meditation on the word of God—the word that nourishes and strengthens, guides and protects; the word that keeps our hearts supple towards the Lord our God and gracious towards all he brings across our path.

A prayer based on Psalm 1

Lord, may your word be my delight this day. Amid the noise of the crowds, help me to hear your call and correction, to discern your ways of truth and life and love. Make me like a tree planted by streams of water, daily rooted, daily renewed. Help me to bear fruit for your kingdom; for the sake of Jesus, my servant king. Amen

41

MONDAY: PROPHET

The Lord your God will raise up for you a prophet like me from among you, from your own people. You must listen to him. For this is what you asked of the Lord your God at Horeb on the day of the assembly when you said, 'Let us not hear the voice of the Lord our God nor see this great fire any more, or we will die.' The Lord said to me: 'What they say is good. I will raise up for them a prophet like you from among their people, and I will put my words in his mouth. He will tell them everything I command him. I myself will call to account anyone who does not listen to my words that the prophet speaks in my name.'

DEUTERONOMY 18:15–19

Then Jesus cried out, 'Those who believe in me do not believe in me only, but in the one who sent me. When they look at me, they see the one who sent me. I have come into the world as a light, so that no one who believes in me should stay in darkness. As for those who hear my words but do not keep them, I do not judge them. For I did not come to judge the world, but to save the world. There is a judge for those who reject me and do not accept my words; the very words I have spoken will condemn them at the last day. For I did not speak on my own, but the Father who sent me commanded me to say all that I have spoken. I

know that his command leads to eternal life. So whatever I say is just what the Father has told me to say.'
JOHN 12:44–50

Among the various leadership roles spelt out in Deuteronomy 16—18, there is one that sits somewhat uncomfortably with the rest. Kings, judges, priests: all have their equivalents in societies across the world, each with their own spheres of influence, each providing a proper check and balance on the power of the others. But the role of the prophet is far harder to pin down. Prophets, by their nature, are often outside the normal structures of governance, largely excluded from the ministries and synods, the councils and committees that discuss and deliberate, plan and strategise. Prophets are frequently eccentric characters, alarmingly tenacious and remarkably free from the constraints that characterise so-called civilised behaviour. The prophet is frequently the voice in the wilderness, the holy irritant, the wild card, the joker in the pack.

Yet despite the often uncomfortable relationship that existed between kings, priests and judges on the one hand and prophets on the other—despite the almost audible groans of a Saul confronted by a Samuel or an Ahab by an Elijah—there is something about the prophet's role that was essential to the spiritual health of ancient Israel and remains essential to the spiritual health of both church and nation today. In part, prophets were the investigative journalists of their time, tuning into God (rather than tapping into phone lines) to expose the follies and failings of their leaders. In part, they were the social commentators, exercising that role through prose, poetry and (on occasions) the most provocative performance art. Yet at the heart of their ministry lay the words, 'Thus says the Lord'. For whether they were reflecting on the past, commenting on the present or predicting the future; whether their message was tough and challenging or warm and comforting, the authority of the prophets lay in their ability to hear God's voice, then pass it on without fear or favour.

A ministry based on 'Thus says the Lord', of course, requires its own checks and balances to ensure that it is not abused by the mad, the sad and the bad; and Deuteronomy 18 itself distinguishes the role of prophet from that of pagan medium, witch and soothsayer, before spelling out some of the principles by which Israel was to separate the true prophets from the false. In practice it must have been difficult to apply those principles whenever a new prophet came to town; but over time, certain individuals rose head and shoulders above their contemporaries when it came to their integrity and courage, their faithfulness to God's word and ability to foresee God's future.

That didn't make prophetic life easy, let alone give prophets an honoured role in society: as Jesus himself pressed on to his final Passover festival, he did so in the full knowledge of what awaited him, 'for surely no prophet can die outside Jerusalem!' (Luke 13:33). But the simple observation that a very large part of the Christian scriptures is given over to the exploits, the sermons and the writings of the prophets suggests that here is an aspect of our tradition that must never be ridiculed, sidelined or excluded. 'Do not treat prophecies with contempt', Paul instructed the church in Thessalonica; 'hold on to what is good, reject whatever is harmful' (1 Thessalonians 5:20–21).

John the Baptist was clearly a prophet—indeed, 'more than a prophet', according to Jesus himself (Matthew 11:9)

—but was he the 'Prophet like Moses' that we read of in Deuteronomy 18? That was one of the questions raised at the beginning of his ministry, and John himself flatly answered, 'No' (John 1:21). Was Jesus *the* Prophet? It certainly looked like it, as both his words and prophetic deeds attested (John 6:14, 7:40; Acts 3:22–24), though the question was never put to him directly. Yet as the crowds began to assemble for the Passover festival that would change the world, Jesus spoke in terms that were reminiscent of the words of Moses all those years before. Here indeed was one who 'did not speak on my own, but the Father who sent me commanded me to say all that I have spoken'. Here was one who must be listened to, for, as Peter had previously recognised with remarkable clarity, 'You have the words of eternal life' (John 6:68).

'Do not treat prophecies with contempt.' It's an important message in a church that all too easily becomes self-serving and institutionalised, and in a world of spiritual famine— 'not a famine of food or a thirst for water', as the prophet Amos put it, 'but a famine of hearing the words of the Lord' (Amos 8:11). In one sense, of course, Jesus, as the Word incarnate, is also God's last word: any 'prophecy' today that contradicts his word is to be firmly rejected. But whatever the checks and balances we wisely put in place, how important that we make room for the prophetic in both church and nation. Councils and committees are all very well, but how we should crave the 'foolishness of God' which is 'wiser than human wisdom', the 'weakness of God' which is 'stronger than human strength' (1 Corinthians 1:25).

A prayer based on 1 Corinthians 14:1–3

Generous Lord, help me to follow in the way of love and to seek the gifts of your Spirit, especially the gift of prophecy. May my life today bring strength, encouragement and comfort to others, for Jesus' sake. Amen

42

TUESDAY: PRIEST

The Lord said to Moses, 'Tell Aaron and his sons, "This is how you are to bless the Israelites. Say to them: 'The Lord bless you and keep you; the Lord make his face shine on you and be gracious to you; the Lord turn his face toward you and give you peace.'" So they will put my name on the Israelites, and I will bless them.'

NUMBERS 6:22–27

After Jesus said this, he looked toward heaven and prayed: 'Father… I have revealed you to those whom you gave me out of the world. They were yours; you gave them to me and they have obeyed your word. Now they know that everything you have given me comes from you. For I gave them the words you gave me and they accepted them. They knew with certainty that I came from you, and they believed that you sent me. I pray for them. I am not praying for the world, but for those you have given me, for they are yours… Holy Father, protect them by the power of your name—the name you gave me—so that they may be one as we are one… For them I sanctify myself, that they too may be truly sanctified. My prayer is not for them alone. I pray also for those who will believe in me through their message, that all of them may be one, Father, just as you are in me

and I am in you… Then the world will know that you sent me and have loved them even as you have loved me.'
JOHN 17:1, 6–11, 19–23 (ABRIDGED)

The priestly blessing in Numbers 6 is one of the most celebrated prayers in the Old Testament and a strong contender for a place in the list of the top ten passages in the Pentateuch. As a poem it is beautifully constructed: a threefold repetition of the word 'Yahweh', followed by sentences that lengthen in Hebrew from three words to five to seven, all culminating in the rich term *shalom* or 'peace'. As a prayer it movingly touches on the themes of God's blessing and protection, his grace and favour, his attentiveness and generosity. As a Christian scripture (as well as a Jewish one), its structure is pleasingly trinitarian.

The idea of blessing has varying connotations in the Old Testament, ranging from the powerful to the polite. When Jacob cheats his brother out of his father's blessing in Genesis 27, for example, it's clear that this event packs a strong spiritual punch; when Boaz greets his harvesters with the words, 'The Lord be with you!' and they respond, 'The Lord bless you!' there's a genuine grace and piety in their exchanges, but little more than that (Ruth 2:4). But when we read the blessing in Numbers 6, we sense its proximity to the powerful end of the spectrum. This isn't Aaron simply sending out a liturgical signal that the service is over and it's time for coffee and biscuits at the back of church. This is Aaron calling down the blessing of God, his power and his presence, upon his people.

Here we are on familiar territory, of course, in our modern understanding of priesthood, for while much of the job description of the priest in Leviticus and Numbers may appear to combine the roles of GP, hygienist and abattoir assistant, the commitment to intercede for God's people and pronounce his blessing upon them remains a strong and enduring mark of the priestly calling today. The promise to protect the health of the people of God (whether physically, spiritually, morally or relationally) is a high priority too, of course—the Christian equivalent of the priest as GP, hygienist and abattoir assistant—but, without the commitment to intercession and blessing, it's hard to recognise an authentic priestly ministry at work. Even Aaron's high priestly robes carried their own message, with the names of the twelve tribes of Israel carved on to two onyx stones attached to the shoulder pads: a symbol of Aaron's prayers for the people and 'a memorial before the Lord' (see Exodus 28:9–13).

It was Clement of Alexandria, in the early fifth century, who first coined the term 'the high priestly prayer' to describe Jesus' powerful intercession in John 17, as the evening in the upper room (the lull before the storm) drew to a close. One of Jesus' phrases in particular—his words, 'For them I sanctify myself'—takes us right back to the days of the exodus and the elaborate rituals by which the high priest would prepare for his duties, especially on the Day of Atonement (see Exodus 30). Jesus' own preparations, though—as great high priest and sacrificial lamb—were anything but ritualistic. Here was the culmination of a whole lifetime of obedience to his heavenly Father. And from that place of obedient, trusting relationship he went on to pray for his disciples (the 'twelve tribes' on his priestly 'garments'), before interceding for the church of the future, the fruit of the disciples' mission.

We cannot begin to do justice to this prayer in such little space—and it would be well worth reading it slowly in its entirety and reflecting on its great themes of eternal life, knowing God, protection, holiness, truth, joy, love and unity. Earlier in the evening, Jesus had promised his peace (John 14:27), his shalom, picking up where Numbers 6 left off; and throughout his prayer the themes of blessing and protection, of grace and favour, of attentiveness and generosity, are never far away, despite an occasion that must have been fraught with tension and fear. Jesus 'always lives to intercede for [us]', proclaimed the author of the letter to the Hebrews (7:25) in a brilliant extended set of variations on the theme of Jesus as our high priest (though one in the line of Melchizedek, not Aaron); and here, in John 17, we get the best possible insight into the heart of Jesus' intercession to his Father.

'You are... a royal priesthood' (1 Peter 2:9): it's a reminder that every Christian is called to this ministry of priestly intercession. And how are we to be blessed and a blessing? What are the priestly robes that we are called upon to wear? As Paul puts it, 'Therefore, as God's chosen people, holy and dearly loved, clothe yourselves with compassion, kindness, humility, gentleness and patience... Let the peace of Christ rule in your hearts, since as members of one body you were called to peace. And be thankful' (Colossians 3:12, 15).

A prayer based on Psalm 67
(to be prayed for ourselves and for the world God loves)

May God be gracious to us and bless us
and make his face shine on us
so that your ways may be known on earth,
your salvation among all nations.
May the peoples praise you, God;
may all the peoples praise you.

May the nations be glad and sing for joy,
for you rule the peoples with equity
and guide the nations of the earth.
May the peoples praise you, God;
may all the peoples praise you.
May God bless us still,
so that all the ends of the earth will fear him. Amen

43

WEDNESDAY: LAMB

Observe the month of Aviv and celebrate the Passover of the Lord your God, because in the month of Aviv he brought you out of Egypt by night. Sacrifice as the Passover to the Lord your God an animal from your flock or herd at the place the Lord will choose as a dwelling for his Name. Do not eat it with bread made with yeast, but for seven days eat unleavened bread, the bread of affliction, because you left Egypt in haste—so that all the days of your life you may remember the time of your departure from Egypt... You must not sacrifice the Passover in any town the Lord your God gives you except in the place he will choose as a dwelling for his Name. There you must sacrifice the Passover in the evening, when the sun goes down, on the anniversary of your departure from Egypt. Roast it and eat it at the place the Lord your God will choose. Then in the morning return to your tents.

DEUTERONOMY 16:1–3, 5–7

The next day John saw Jesus coming toward him and said, 'Look, the Lamb of God, who takes away the sin of the world!'

JOHN 1:29

'"The fire and wood are here," Isaac said, "but where is the lamb for the burnt offering?" Abraham answered, "God himself will provide the lamb for the burnt offering, my son." And the two of them went on together' (Genesis 22:7–8)

It's perhaps the most haunting and heart-wrenching image in the whole Old Testament: the sight of a father and his son climbing a mountain, the father believing (with good reason) that God is calling him to sacrifice his boy. The tribes among whom Abraham lived practised such human sacrifices: the cult of the Ammonite god Molech comes in for particular censure in this regard (see, for example, Leviticus 18:21). But here, for a terrifying moment, it seemed as though Molech and the God of Abraham were somehow in league. 'God himself will provide the lamb for the burnt offering,' stated Abraham—and that 'lamb', he firmly believed, would be none other than Isaac himself.

In the event, as we know, God had no intention of allowing the human sacrifice to go ahead—and a ram was duly provided as a burnt offering to take Isaac's place (Genesis 22:13). But these linked ideas of sacrificial lambs, of God's provision and of a remarkable reprieve from the imposition of the death penalty work their way through the entire scriptures from Genesis to Revelation.

It's during the account of Passover night in Exodus 12 that these themes next congregate: the firstborn of the Israelites are reprieved from the sentence imposed on their Egyptian contemporaries as a lamb is slaughtered and its blood is sprinkled on the doorframes of their houses. Since this was the moment that finally broke through Pharaoh's stubborn defences, catapulting Israel out of centuries of Egyptian enslavement, it's hardly surprising that the Passover feast came to symbolise considerably more than just an event in Israel's distant past. 'Why is this night different from all other nights?' asks a child at the Passover seder even today, and the answer rehearses the harshness of Israel's slavery and the glory of her liberation, all masterminded by the mighty Yahweh himself.

This move from one-off event to annual festival is already in evidence in Exodus 12 but is given added impetus in today's reading from Deuteronomy 16. By the time of its writing, the feasts of Passover and unleavened bread had become one. By now, some concessions had been granted to Israel's herdsmen, allowing a wider range of animals to be sacrificed during the festivities. But perhaps the most interesting part of this passage is the link it makes between the historic story of the exodus and the future establishment of the temple in Jerusalem. It may remind us of Paul's account of the last supper, the Christian Passover meal, with its principal focus on the past combined with an expectant eye to the future: 'For whenever you eat this bread and drink this cup, you proclaim the Lord's death until he comes' (1 Corinthians 11:26).

'Look, the Lamb of God, who takes away the sin of the world': John the evangelist couldn't wait until the last supper to convey this truth to us, placing John the Baptist's startling revelation in the very first chapter of his Gospel. Behind the Baptist's insight lay the story of Abraham, with the words of this great man of faith now cast in a deeply prophetic light: 'God himself will provide the lamb for the burnt offering, my son.' Behind it, too, lay the Passover story and the establishment of Israel's temple worship, with animal sacrifice apparently at its core. The so-called 'servant songs' of Isaiah the prophet had also added powerfully to the vocabulary of sacrificial lambs, of God's provision, of what the theologians call 'substitutionary atonement': 'He was led like a lamb to the slaughter, and as a sheep before its shearers is silent, so he did not open his mouth' (53:7); 'We all, like sheep, have gone astray, each of us has turned to his own way; and the Lord has laid on him the iniquity of us all' (v. 6).

And it was against this profound theological backdrop that John pointed out a young man to his disciples one day, indicating that here was none other than the Lamb of God, one whose sacrificial death would bring God's liberation from a far older, darker enslavement than that imposed by the Pharaohs: here was God's provision to deal with the slavery of sin and death, and to do so not simply for the people of Israel but for the world in its entirety.

As we approach the climax of Holy Week—as the Lamb of God moves patiently and steadily towards his executioners—a proper response is one of the deepest worship. In the book of Revelation it's precisely the sight of this 'Lamb who was slain' that inspires the glorious new songs of the four living creatures, the 24 elders, the 'angels, numbering thousands upon thousands, and ten thousand times ten thousand' and 'every creature in heaven and on earth and under the earth and on the sea, and all that is in them' (5:6–14). You could hardly imagine a larger or more impressive choir than that!

Worship, though, is more than just singing: it includes a living of our entire lives to God's praise and glory. In the words of Paul, 'Christ, our Passover lamb, has been sacrificed. Therefore let us keep the Festival, not with the old bread leavened with malice and wickedness, but with the un-leavened bread of sincerity and truth' (1 Corinthians 5:7–8).

A hymn based on the songs of Revelation 5

Worthy is the Lamb, who was slain,
to receive power and wealth and wisdom and strength
and honour and glory and praise!
To him who sits on the throne and to the Lamb
be praise and honour and glory and power,
for ever and ever! Amen

44

MAUNDY THURSDAY: SHEPHERD

Moses said to the Lord, 'May the Lord, the God of every human spirit, appoint someone over this community to go out and come in before them, one who will lead them out and bring them in, so the Lord's people will not be like sheep without a shepherd.'

NUMBERS 27:15–17

[Jesus said] 'Very truly I tell you... anyone who does not enter the sheepfold by the gate, but climbs in by some other way, is a thief and a robber. The one who enters by the gate is the shepherd of the sheep. The gatekeeper opens the gate for him, and the sheep listen to his voice. He calls his own sheep by name and leads them out. When he has brought out all his own, he goes on ahead of them, and his sheep follow him because they know his voice. But they will never follow a stranger; in fact, they will run away from him because they do not recognise a stranger's voice.' ... Jesus said again, 'Very truly I tell you, I am the gate for the sheep. All who have come before me are thieves and robbers, but the sheep have not listened to them. I am the gate; whoever enters through me will be saved. They will come in and go out, and find pasture. The thief comes only to steal and kill and destroy; I have come that they may have life, and have it to the full. I am the good shepherd. The good shepherd lays down his life for the sheep... I have other sheep that are not of this sheepfold. I must bring them also. They too will listen to my voice, and there shall be one flock and one shepherd.'

JOHN 10:1–5, 7–11, 16

'Like sheep without a shepherd': it is a haunting phrase, speaking of lostness, vulnerability, a lack of common purpose and direction, even potential anarchy; and to Moses (who had spent many years working as a shepherd himself), the prospect of a leaderless Israel was every bit as alarming as a completely unguarded flock. The prophet Isaiah later picked up the theme to describe the Babylon of his day (13:14); closer to home, the prophets Micaiah and Ezekiel used it to criticise the godless leadership of Israel and Judah respectively (1 Kings 22:17; Ezekiel 34:5); and as Jesus surveyed the huge and disconsolate crowds who had followed John the Baptist into the desert, and had now just learnt of his execution, we're told that 'he had compassion on them, because they were like sheep without a shepherd' (Mark 6:34).

Moses used another intriguing phrase as he prepared Israel for the handover of leadership to his protégé Joshua, saying that here was a shepherd who would 'go out and come in before [the community]', one who would 'lead them out and bring them in'. In terms of the exodus story, Moses had fulfilled half of that mandate, leading God's people out of Egypt, but it would take a second shepherd, Joshua, to complete the job and bring them into the promised land.

Jesus' description of himself as the 'good shepherd' is one of the best-loved passages in John's Gospel, picking up on

Numbers 27 and on the rich heritage of sheep and shepherd imagery across the Old Testament. The shepherd in Jesus' day had nicknames for his sheep and developed an extraordinary symbiotic relationship with them. At night, up on the hillside, he would lead his flock into a roughly constructed sheepfold before lying down at its entrance to keep the sheep in and predators out. The prophet Ezekiel had developed similar themes, contrasting the self-interested bad shepherds of his day with a selfless vision of good shepherding (ch. 34); and here, in Jesus, was the perfect model of that good shepherd—attentive, friendly, compassionate, courageous.

'The good shepherd lays down his life for his sheep': this was the one jarring note in Jesus' description. It's true that previous Bible passages had emphasised the bravery required in shepherding—the tussles with lions and bears, for example, to which David famously alluded in his interview with Saul (see 1 Samuel 17:34–36)—but the idea of a shepherd 'laying down his life' for the flock was radically new. On the surface it seemed a ridiculous idea, too: sacrificial lambs are all very well, but what on earth is the use of a sacrificial shepherd? Yet Jesus' talk of gathering 'other sheep that are not of this sheepfold' spoke of a future beyond the laying down of his life, pointing forward to the resurrection and the church's subsequent mission to the Gentiles.

According to John, Jesus' teaching was delivered during the feast of Tabernacles, but one Greek word links this passage to the events of the first Maundy Thursday, as Jesus gathered his disciples together for one last meal before his death. The word is *tithesin*, and it means 'lays down': for, just as Jesus the good shepherd prepared to 'lay down his life' for the sheep, so Jesus the loving servant 'lay down' his outer clothing as he stooped to wash his disciples' feet

(13:4). John uses this word on another occasion, too. At the wedding in Cana of Galilee, the master of the banquet called the bridegroom aside with the words, 'Everyone "lays down" the choice wine first and then the cheaper wine after the guests have had too much to drink' (2:10). And so the themes of shepherd, servant, sacrifice and the choice wine of the kingdom are brought together in John's rich commentary on this holiest of seasons.

Laying down our lives; lying at the entrance of the sheepfold: these are powerful images, especially when we remember that we are the body of Christ, called to share in his shepherdly ministry today. It's true that pastors, church leaders, have a particular responsibility in this regard; yet every Christian is called to keep the sheep in and predators out, whether the sheepfold is our church or family, our workplace, community or friendship group.

And that is why Paul's parting words to the Ephesian elders are well worth every Christian reflecting on as Good Friday approaches: 'Keep watch over yourselves and all the flock of which the Holy Spirit has made you overseers. Be shepherds of the church of God, which he bought with his own blood' (Acts 20:28).

A blessing for ourselves and our flock, based on Hebrews 13

May the God of peace, who through the blood of the eternal covenant brought back from the dead our Lord Jesus, that great Shepherd of the sheep, equip us with everything good for doing his will, and may he work in us what is pleasing to him, through Jesus Christ, to whom be glory for ever and ever. Amen

45

GOOD FRIDAY: SALVATION

[The Israelites] travelled from Mount Hor along the route to the Red Sea, to go around Edom. But the people grew impatient on the way; they spoke against God and against Moses, and said, 'Why have you brought us up out of Egypt to die in the wilderness? There is no bread! There is no water! And we detest this miserable food!' Then the Lord sent venomous snakes among them; they bit the people and many Israelites died. The people came to Moses and said, 'We sinned when we spoke against the Lord and against you. Pray that the Lord will take the snakes away from us.' So Moses prayed for the people. The Lord said to Moses, 'Make a snake and put it up on a pole; anyone who is bitten can look at it and live.' So Moses made a bronze snake and put it up on a pole. Then when anyone was bitten by a snake and looked at the bronze snake, they lived.

NUMBERS 21:4–9

[Jesus said]: 'No one has ever gone into heaven except the one who came from heaven—the Son of Man. Just as Moses lifted up the snake in the wilderness, so the Son of Man must be lifted up, that everyone who believes may have eternal life in him.' For God so loved the world that he gave his one and only Son, that whoever believes in him shall not perish but have eternal life. For God did not send his Son into the world to condemn the world, but to save the world through him.

JOHN 3:13–17

It might seem irreverent to compare the bronze snake in today's readings with the formaldehyde-drenched sheep and sharks of British artist Damien Hirst, but there's something about the last of the grumbling stories in the desert wanderings that retains a similar power to divide, to provoke and to shock.

On the one hand, the construction of a 'snake on a stick' seems to have been clearly commanded by God, and the Israelites who looked at the snake were equally clearly healed. Jesus himself referred positively to this story in his conversation with leading rabbi Nicodemus, and the image (together with its equivalent in Greek mythology) has since been adopted by the World Health Organisation and a host of other medical bodies.

On the other hand, the snake was an apparent breach of the second commandment, and caused considerable trouble in future years as an object of Israel's worship, leading good king Hezekiah to destroy it as part of his wide-ranging temple reforms (2 Kings 18:4). The apocryphal Wisdom of Solomon sought to dampen down the controversy by wisely stressing that 'the one who turned towards [the snake] was saved, not by the thing that was beheld, but by you, the Saviour of all' (16:7, NRSV); but the use of the snake in Egyptian iconology (together with the archaeological discovery of a small metal snake in a Midianite shrine) has led some commentators to believe that Moses was here being shaped by his Egyptian upbringing and the culture of his Midianite father-in-law, as much as by his allegiance to the Lord his God.

From a Christian perspective it's impossible to read this passage without reference to that night when Nicodemus came to Jesus, confused but intrigued by what he was seeing and hearing. To Nicodemus' somewhat clumsy questioning, Jesus cryptically responded, 'Just as Moses lifted up the snake in the wilderness, so the Son of Man must be lifted up, that everyone who believes may have eternal life in him.'

It wasn't just at this early stage in Jesus' ministry that the 'snake-on-a-stick' made its presence felt, either. On two later occasions (John 8:28; 12:32) Jesus spoke of his calling to be 'lifted up', a faint echo of the story in the desert, as well as of the greatest of Isaiah's servant songs (Isaiah 52:13—53:12). And while other Bible writers later used the same word to refer to Jesus' ascension and exaltation (for example, Acts 2:33; 5:31; Philippians 2:9), there's no question that, for Jesus himself, the 'lifting up' was a reference to the cross. With humankind stricken with the venom of sin, only the death of the Son of Man could provide healing, salvation and eternal life.

The full implications of 'Jesus as snake' will be worked through in tomorrow's readings. But as we survey the wondrous cross today; as we stand back to witness the most bloody and brutal of executions carried out on the most godly and compassionate of human beings, we see a sight whose ability to divide, to provoke and to shock makes the bronze snake and the works of Damien Hirst seem positively tame by comparison. 'Jews demand signs and Greeks look for wisdom' (to quote Paul again), 'but we preach Christ crucified: a stumbling block to Jews and foolishness to Gentiles, but to those whom God has called... Christ the power of God and the wisdom of God' (1 Corinthians 1:22–

24). Closer to our own day, the controversy surrounding Mel Gibson's alarmingly realistic (if sometimes overstated) *The Passion of the Christ*[19] also reminds us of the truly shocking nature of the events of that first Good Friday.

It's important here that we don't fall into the idolatry that made the bronze snake into a talisman, then an object of worship. It's not the cross that saves us; it is rather 'Christ crucified', and any religion that exalts the cross without doing business with the Christ is mere superstition. But it's as we acknowledge the dangerous, even deadly, nature of the sin that separates us from God our heavenly Father; as we humble ourselves before him in the recognition that he has every right to condemn our attitudes and our actions; as we long to know that reality so beautifully expressed in the line from one of the greatest of all hymns—'ransomed, healed, restored, forgiven'[20]—that the Father gently directs our eyes towards his Son with the promise that 'anyone who is bitten can look at [him] and live'.

The snake served two objectives in the story from the desert: as an agent of God's punishment and an agent of God's healing. So what was God's objective in the coming and the crucifixion of the Son of Man? Was it punishment or healing? In the glorious and far-reaching words of John 3:17, addressed to all who would 'look at him' in repentance and faith, 'God did not send his Son into the world to condemn the world, but to save the world through him.'

A prayer of response from a hymn by Isaac Watts

Were the whole realm of nature mine,
That were an offering far too small;
Love so amazing, so divine,
Demands my soul, my life, my all.[21]

46

HOLY SATURDAY: CORPSE

'If anyone guilty of a capital offence is put to death and
their body is exposed on a pole, you must not leave the
body hanging on the pole overnight. Be sure to bury it that
same day, because anyone who is hung on a pole is under
God's curse. You must not desecrate the land the Lord your
God is giving you as an inheritance.'

DEUTERONOMY 21:22–23

Now it was the day of Preparation, and the next day was
to be a special Sabbath. Because the Jewish leaders did not
want the bodies left on the crosses during the Sabbath,
they asked Pilate to have the legs broken and the bodies
taken down... Later, Joseph of Arimathea asked Pilate for
the body of Jesus. Now Joseph was a disciple of Jesus,
but secretly because he feared the Jewish leaders. With
Pilate's permission, he came and took the body away. He
was accompanied by Nicodemus, the man who earlier had
visited Jesus at night. Nicodemus brought a mixture of
myrrh and aloes, about thirty-five kilograms. Taking Jesus'
body, the two of them wrapped it, with the spices, in strips
of linen. This was in accordance with Jewish burial customs.
At the place where Jesus was crucified, there was a garden,
and in the garden a new tomb, in which no one had ever

been laid. Because it was the Jewish day of Preparation and since the tomb was nearby, they laid Jesus there.

JOHN 19:31, 38–42

'By the seventh day God had finished the work he had been doing; so on the seventh day he rested from all his work' (Genesis 2:2).

There's something refreshing and restful about Holy Saturday, the 'special Sabbath', the seventh day of Holy Week—and not just for church leaders coming up for air between the heart-wrenching rigours of Good Friday and the joyful rigours of Easter Day.

Jesus' last word from the cross in John's Gospel was a single Greek term, translated 'It is finished!' (19:30), and for those with ears to hear, the 'finished' word takes us right back to the beginning of the book of Genesis, where God had 'finished the work he had been doing' by the end of Friday, the evening of the sixth day.

God's final act before embarking on his sabbath rest had been the creation of humankind—a development that (along with the rest of his creation) he had deemed 'very good'. Yet the events of Good Friday showed humanity at its worst—the sorriest catalogue of betrayal, cowardice, jealousy, violence and hatred imaginable. Only one man emerged unscathed from the wreckage (we might think perhaps of Pilate's 'Here is the man!' in John 19:5)—unscathed, that is, apart from his body, which had been scathed almost beyond recognition. Only Jesus retained a steadfast integrity, a 'very good'-ness throughout the whole messy affair. And now he was dying, his body hanging there on the cross; and it was Friday afternoon, late on the sixth day.

There was a stipulation in the book of Deuteronomy that

an executed body should not remain hanging overnight but should be buried the same day. This contrasted strongly (and humanely) with the normal Roman practice of taking down their crucified victims and leaving their bodies to the mercy of the vultures and dogs. Since the next day was the sabbath (and the Passover to boot), the Jewish leaders foresaw a problem in keeping both the sabbath law and this stipulation from Deuteronomy simultaneously. As a result, they persuaded the Roman authorities to smash the victims' legs with a mallet so as to ensure that their bodies could be dealt with before the sabbath dawned. Jesus' legs, however, were not shattered. As a sword thrust into his side confirmed, he was already dead.

Here, if anywhere, is the very worst example of that tendency among certain of Jesus' contemporaries to get their priorities all wrong, to 'strain out a gnat but swallow a camel', in Jesus' memorable phrase (Matthew 23:24): killing the Son of God before observing all the legal niceties in the disposal of his body. Yet just as we are at our most despairing in our reflections on fallen human nature (or in the greatest danger of pinning it all on 'The Jews' or their leadership), two men from the heart of the Jewish establishment step out of the shadows to perform an act of extraordinary generosity and courage. One was a Pharisee—Nicodemus, who popped up in yesterday's reading (and once more in John 7:50–51). The other was a fellow member of the Jewish ruling council (and a fellow dissenter to the council's decision to have Jesus executed)—a man called Joseph of Arimathea. Between them, these men risked the wrath of their religious contemporaries and the violence of the Roman authorities to secure the body of Jesus and ensure its proper entombment.

Less than a week earlier, Mary of Bethany had famously

229

poured a jar of expensive oil on Jesus' feet, and Jesus had responded with both gratitude and (perhaps) a little sense of regret: 'It was intended that she should save this perfume for the day of my burial' (John 12:7). But if Mary had somehow jumped the gun, Joseph was there to take her place. A full 35 kilograms (75 pounds) of precious spices, enough to anoint a king, were lavished on the body of Jesus before that body was wrapped and placed in its final resting place—or such was the view of the two courageous men as the stone was rolled across its entrance.

Then, to paraphrase Genesis, 'by the seventh day [Jesus] had finished the work he had been doing; so on the seventh day he rested from all his work'.

So what was the work that Jesus had been doing? Why the gruesome spectacle of the cross with this human 'snake-on-a-stick'? The same passage of Deuteronomy that stipulates the correct treatment of the body of an executed criminal also contains the teaching that 'anyone who is hung on a pole is under God's curse'. It's a verse that the early church was quick to recognise as a remarkable insight into the death of Jesus (see Acts 5:30; 10:39), and it chimed in too with the picture of Jesus as snake, given the strongly negative connotations of that image from the garden of Eden onwards. 'Christ redeemed us from the curse of the law by becoming a curse for us,' writes Paul in Galatians 3:13; or, as Peter put it: 'He himself bore our sins in his body on the tree, so that we might die to sins and live for righteousness; by his wounds you have been healed' (1 Peter 2:24).

What work, then, was 'finished' on the cross (as we look with the benefit of post-Easter-morning hindsight)? Simply the possibility of our forgiveness, healing and restoration— the possibility of a 'new creation' (2 Corinthians 5:17), where God could once again contemplate humankind and declare it 'very good'. And perhaps Nicodemus and Joseph of Arimathea, in their generosity and courage, give us our first insights into what this new creation might look like.

A prayer based on words attributed to Bernard of Clairvaux

What language shall I borrow
To thank thee, dearest friend,
For this thy dying sorrow,
Thy pity without end?
O make me thine forever;
And should I fainting be,
Lord, let me never, never
Outlive my love for thee.
TRANS. JAMES ALEXANDER (1830)

47

EASTER DAY: FULFILMENT

Early in the morning Joshua and all the Israelites set out...
and went to the Jordan, where they camped before crossing
over... Joshua told the people, 'Consecrate yourselves, for
tomorrow the Lord will do amazing things among you.'
... So when the people broke camp to cross the Jordan,
the priests carrying the ark of the covenant went ahead of
them. Now the Jordan is at flood stage all during harvest.
Yet as soon as the priests who carried the ark reached the
Jordan and their feet touched the water's edge, the water
from upstream stopped flowing... The priests who carried
the ark of the covenant of the Lord stopped in the middle of
the Jordan and stood on dry ground, while all Israel passed
by until the whole nation had completed the crossing on
dry ground.

JOSHUA 3:1, 5, 14–17 (ABRIDGED)

Early on the first day of the week, while it was still dark,
Mary Magdalene went to the tomb and saw that the stone
had been removed from the entrance. So she came running
to Simon Peter and the other disciple, the one Jesus loved,
and said, 'They have taken the Lord out of the tomb, and
we don't know where they have put him!'... [Later] Mary
stood outside the tomb crying. As she wept, she bent over
to look into the tomb and saw two angels in white, seated

where Jesus' body had been, one at the head and the other at the foot. They asked her, 'Woman, why are you crying?' 'They have taken my Lord away,' she said, 'and I don't know where they have put him.' At this, she turned around and saw Jesus standing there, but she did not realise that it was Jesus. He asked her, 'Woman, why are you crying? Who is it you are looking for?' Thinking he was the gardener, she said, 'Sir, if you have carried him away, tell me where you have put him, and I will get him.' Jesus said to her, 'Mary.' She turned toward him and cried out in Aramaic, 'Rabboni!' (which means 'Teacher'). Jesus said, 'Do not hold on to me, for I have not yet ascended to the Father. Go instead to my brothers and tell them, "I am ascending to my Father and your Father, to my God and your God."' Mary Magdalene went to the disciples with the news: 'I have seen the Lord!'
JOHN 20:1–2, 11–18

The promised land; a 'land flowing with milk and honey'; a 'single cluster of grapes' that takes two grown men to carry it (Numbers 13:23); a 'good land' overrunning with 'wheat and barley, vines and fig trees, pomegranates, olive oil and honey' where 'bread will not be scarce and you will lack nothing' (Deuteronomy 8:8–9): this was the vision that had helped to sustain the Israelites through the 40 years of their desert wanderings. And now the vision was within their reach. Moses had led the flock out, and Joshua his successor was to bring them in. Only the River Jordan stood between God's people and God's inheritance.

Back at the beginning of the exodus, Moses had stretched his hand out over the sea and the waters had parted (Exodus 14:21). But on this occasion it was not Joshua who took centre stage; it was rather the ark of the covenant—that beautiful, potent symbol of the presence of God constructed by Bezalel and his assistant four decades earlier (Exodus 37:1–9). And as the priests carried the ark into the river, the water stopped flowing, allowing this marathon of a journey to reach its destination at last. It wasn't strictly a miracle, perhaps: we know of three subsequent occasions (the latest in 1927) when a landslide blocked the river in exactly the place mentioned in Joshua 3. But the timing of the living God in using such an event to bring together his chosen people and his promised land was, of course, quite perfect.

If a river was the obstacle for Joshua, it was a rock that threatened to thwart Mary Magdalene: a large, heavy stone rolled across the entrance of the garden tomb once Nicodemus and Joseph had completed their ministrations at the end of the sixth day. The seventh day—a sabbath rest—had come and gone: unlike the Israelites in Joshua's time, Jesus' disciples had had no inkling that 'tomorrow the Lord will do amazing things among you'; and very early on the first day of a new week, Mary had made her way to the tomb to mourn and to pray.

Mary's first thoughts on discovering the gaping hole at the entrance of the tomb were certainly not that some great miracle had occurred. Remembering the quantity of spices wrapped round Jesus' body, she probably thought of grave robbers or of meddling Roman bureaucrats or even of the perpetrators of some sick joke. Deeply upset, she ran back to the disciples, two of whom then went to see for themselves.

It was only as she later returned to the tomb and looked inside that Mary first became aware of a mysterious angelic presence, and then of a man standing behind her. Perhaps he was the gardener, Mary thought, and in one sense he was—the 'new Adam', as Tom Wright puts it, 'the gardener, charged with bringing the chaos of God's creation into new order, into flower, into fruitfulness'.[22] And it was as the gardener and good shepherd called Mary by name that the astonishing truth finally dawned on her. Running back to the disciples once more, she became the first witness to the resurrection—the 'apostle to the apostles', as she was later known—blurting out in her awestruck, breathless enthusiasm, 'I have seen the Lord!'

And as we put together the stories of the old exodus and the new exodus for the last time, it is right to see this risen Jesus as the new Joshua, not least because, in Hebrew, the two names are the same. Yet as Mary and John and the other disciples later came to recognise, it wasn't enough to picture Jesus in this light. He was Joshua, yes, but he was also the ark of the covenant, the very presence of God himself, leading all who would follow him through the deep waters of death and into the glories of life eternal.

'It was impossible for death to keep its hold on him,' Peter would soon be proclaiming when the next major Jewish festival, the Day of Pentecost, came round (Acts 2:24). Of course it was. For here, in Peter's earlier words, was none other than 'the Christ, the Son of the living God' (Matthew 16:16). And as this risen Christ met with Mary, as he affectionately spoke of the disciples as 'my brothers' and of God as 'my Father and your Father', so the vistas of a glorious new landscape began to open up before her—this promised land of restored relationships, of peace with God, of joy and hope and reconciliation, both now and into all eternity. In the later, spine-tingling words of Paul, 'No eye has seen, no ear has heard, no mind has conceived what God has prepared for those who love him' (1 Corinthians 2:9).

A prayer, based on the hymn 'Thine be the glory' by Edmond Budry

No more we doubt thee, glorious Prince of life;
life is naught without thee; aid us in our strife;
make us more than conquerors, through thy deathless love:
bring us safe through Jordan to thy home above.
Thine be the glory, risen conquering Son,
Endless is the vict'ry, thou o'er death hast won!
TRANS. RICHARD HOYLE (1925)

A FINAL BLESSING

The Lord bless you and keep you;
The Lord make his face to shine on you, and be gracious to you;
The Lord lift up his countenance upon you, and give you peace.

NUMBERS 6:24–26 (RSV)

LENT GROUP
DISCUSSION GUIDE

Where this book is used in a small group setting, members should be encouraged to read the relevant chapters on a daily basis and to come with any thoughts and insights they may have picked up along the way. This may well raise issues for further discussion, into which these additional Bible passages, questions and prayer suggestions can be incorporated.

'Week' 1 in fact covers eleven days (from Ash Wednesday to the second Saturday in Lent), with Weeks 2–5 covering seven days each as normal, and Week 6 running through from Palm Sunday to Easter Day itself. If groups meet midweek, their leaders may wish to omit any questions that relate to chapters that won't have been read by the time the group convenes.

Reference to 'chapters' in this discussion guide relate to chapters in the book and not in the Bible.

Week 1: Provision in the desert

Read Ephesians 1:3–14.

1. The book's first chapters focus on the ways in which God met the Israelites' obvious needs for food and water, alongside less obvious ones, such as worship and vision. Are there any lessons that have particularly struck us so far?

2. How does Paul fill out this picture of God's provision in Ephesians 1:3–14? If we were to choose just one word in this outpouring of praise, what would it be and why?

3. The Israelites may have been enslaved in Egypt, but at least they usually knew where their next meal was coming from. In the desert, they were entirely dependent on Jehovah Jireh, the Lord who provides. When were you last entirely dependent on God to provide? How did it feel, and what was the outcome?

4. Grumbling is a frequent feature of these early chapters in the story of the exodus (and see James 5:9). Why does the Lord seem to take quite such a dim view of it? When are we most tempted to grumble, and what's the antidote?

5. What challenge might Jethro bring, were he to visit our church (see chapter 7)? How might leadership be better shared in the life of the fellowship?

6. Paul has an extraordinary vision of God's plan of salvation, just as vision is part of Moses' experience on Mount Sinai (see chapter 8). Would we live our lives differently if our vision of God (and of his call on our lives) were clearer? How might we respond to the challenge in chapter 8 to 'climb a mountain'?

7. Paul calls us to 'give thanks in all circumstances' (1 Thessalonians 5:18). As you look back over the past 24 hours, write down ten things for which you'd like to give thanks to God—and then do just that, quietly or as a group. Making this a daily discipline would really help us to turn our grumbling into gratitude.

Week 2: God in the desert

Read Ephesians 1:15–23; 3:14–21.

1. Week 2 looks at the lessons that the Israelites learnt about the nature of God after the golden calf disaster. At what period in your life have you grown most in your understanding of the character of God?

2. Chapter 13 focuses on the theme of God's presence with his people. Have we been especially aware of God's presence with us at any point in the last week? How might we better 'practise the presence of God'—in other words, recognise the times when he's at work in and around us?

3. Paul's two great prayers in his letter to the Ephesians teach us much about God's character and purposes, as revealed through Jesus Christ. Is there anything that especially struck us as those prayers were being read?

4. Chapter 14 contrasts the way of covenant with the worship of choice. What are the advantages of living from a place of covenant? How might we respond to a friend or family member who says that they don't want to be 'tied down' in their faith or relationships?

5. 'Jealousy' is often seen as a negative word. How do you relate to the idea of God as a 'jealous God', as explored in chapter 15? Can you think of a situation when you have known a 'godly jealousy' on behalf of yourself or others?

6. Why does holiness sometimes get such a bad press (think of the phrases 'holy Joe' and 'holier than thou')? How might we recapture both the glory of this word and the down-to-earth holiness as explored in chapter 16?

7. Paul's prayer in Ephesians 1:17—that 'the God of our Lord Jesus Christ… may give you the Spirit of wisdom

and revelation, so that you may know him better'—is a wonderful example of how we should pray for those we know and love. In a few moments of quiet, think of someone who especially needs that Spirit of wisdom and revelation at this time. Then quietly pray this prayer on their behalf, and resolve to do so daily in the week ahead.

Week 3: Love in the desert

Read Ephesians 4:1–6; 4:25—5:2.

1. The Israelites were taught to 'live a life of love' during their time in the desert—the focus of Week 3 of our journey through Lent. What most gets in the way of us living a life of love? How might we change that?

2. What does 'loving God' really mean? And how do the words 'heart', 'mind', 'soul' and 'strength' fill out the picture?

3. Today's readings from Paul's letter to the Ephesians help us to explore the theme of 'loving our neighbour', especially in the life of the church. What phrase most challenges us in these instructions? What would be the impact, were our church to embrace them wholeheartedly?

4. Chapter 21 relates the deliberate inefficiency of the gleaning principle to our use of time. Are we in danger of developing an approach to life where there are no 'ragged edges'—'no time for listening, for loving, even for apparently "wasting time" with others (or with God)'? How might we put that right, without losing a proper efficiency and focus?

5. Chapter 22 points towards the vision of a church that is a 'model of intergenerational respect, encouragement and learning'. How might this vision be better realised in the life of our church, while giving due weight to the

particular needs of the young, the elderly, and all points in between?

6. Leviticus 25 connects the themes of compassion for the poor and care for the environment (see chapter 25). How might we seek to respond to these themes in our own life and discipleship?

7. Paul challenges us to 'live a life of love, just as Christ loved us and gave himself up for us as a fragrant offering and sacrifice to God' (Ephesians 5:2). Take a few moments to reflect on the cross—on all that Christ has done for you—then pray that the Spirit of Jesus might fill your life afresh, renewing your love for God, for your neighbour, for the poor and for creation.

Week 4: Lessons from the desert

Read Ephesians 6:10–20.

1. Week 4 takes us from Mount Sinai to within sight of the promised land—a period characterised by turmoil and a critical loss of nerve. As we reflect on the Israelites' rejection of Caleb's and Joshua's minority report, when are we most vulnerable to fear? Is there a situation we are currently facing where the 'giants' loom larger than the 'grapes', and where we're in danger of leaving God out of the equation?

2. Chapter 26 found Moses isolated and in need of a deeper personal and spiritual support. Is our personal and spiritual support adequate at the moment? How might it be strengthened further?

3. What does it mean to 'fear God' (see chapter 29)? How (if at all) might a proper fear of God be 'the perfect antidote to human panic'?

4. Moses' marriage to a Cushite woman caused outrage to his brother and sister, but the Lord took Moses' side (see chapter 27). How can we keep a proper perspective in areas of moral integrity, holding to God's word while rejecting the way of pharisaic pettiness?

5. Today's reading from Ephesians addresses Moses and the Israelites' embattled state. How aware are we of the 'devil's schemes' right now? How might we better protect ourselves in the face of fear, temptation, discouragement and stress?

6. The discussion in chapter 31 concludes with the words, 'If even Moses could be turned into a mean-minded little tyrant, it could happen to anyone.' How might we better support our leaders, especially when we see them close to breaking point?

7. Ephesians 6 introduces us to the 'full armour of God'. Quietly read verses 10–18 once again, prayerfully 'putting on' the various pieces of gospel armour as you prepare yourself for the week ahead. You might like to repeat this exercise as you get dressed each morning.

Week 5: Beyond the desert

Read Ephesians 2:1–10.

1. Moses' sermons in the book of Deuteronomy are the focus of Week 5—teaching designed to prepare the Israelites for their future life in the promised land. Why is it important that we regularly 'set our hearts on things above' (Colossians 3:1)? How can we become 'too earthly minded to be of any heavenly use'?

2. Moses' biggest anxiety was that the promised land would test the Israelites' faith more than the desert had (see

chapter 34). Why is 'affluenza' so often a problem when times are good?

3. In today's reading from Ephesians, Paul draws a parallel between the storyline of the exodus (from slavery to freedom) and the experience of the Christian believer. Is there anything in this passage that especially strikes you, in its depiction of the past, the present or the future?

4. Chapters 35 and 36 describe two ways in which the Israelites were to stick together—through common festivals and a common story. How might we recapture a sense that our story is part of a far bigger story? As we look back, what has been our most joyful and meaningful experience of celebrating a Christian festival?

5. What does Moses' pithy soundbite 'Now choose life' mean for you (see chapter 37)? Why might we choose anything else?

6. What can we learn from the way Moses passed the leadership baton on to Joshua (chapter 38)? How does that compare with your own experience of receiving a fresh responsibility or giving one to someone else?

7. Moses played a key part in God's purposes and left behind a remarkable legacy of integrity, humility and wise and effective leadership. Take some time to reflect on the legacy you would wish to leave behind when you climb that final 'mountain'; and pray that your life on earth would be as fruitful as it possibly can be.

Holy Week: The cross in the desert

Read Ephesians 2:11–22.

1. We follow Jesus' progress through Holy Week with a series of readings from John's Gospel, and look at the roots of much of Jesus' thinking in the story of Israel's desert wanderings. Why did God go to so much trouble to prepare his people for the coming of Jesus? What might have been the content of Jesus' Bible study on the road to Emmaus, when 'beginning with Moses and the Prophets' he 'explained to them what was said in all the Scriptures concerning himself' (Luke 24:27)?

2. Today's reading from Ephesians beautifully fills out our understanding of the events of Holy Week. What does Paul mean by the phrase '[Christ] is our peace'? What is the scope of the peace that Jesus has won for us?

3. Why is it important for leaders to be under authority before they can properly be in authority (chapter 40)? Why is a 'daily discipline of meditation on the word of God' so important—and how might we increasingly build this discipline into our lives?

4. Who are the 'prophets' in today's world (chapter 41)? How is the gift of prophecy best expressed in the life of our church?

5. What does it mean to be a 'royal priesthood' today (chapter 42)? Whose names are carved on the 'onyx stones' of our priestly 'garments', and how might we pray for them more faithfully and consistently?

6. Chapters 43–45 introduce us to three pictures of Jesus' death: Jesus as lamb, good shepherd and snake. How do we respond to these ancient images? How does each of

them help to shed further light on our understanding of the cross?

7. A number of well-known hymns pick up the parallels between Israel's desert wanderings and our life as Christian disciples, including 'Thine be the glory' and 'Guide me, O Thou great Jehovah'. Take one of these hymns and quietly reflect on it for a few minutes; then, how about reciting or singing it together in preparation for Easter?

NOTES

1   The title of a Christmas song written by Kim Gannon and Walter Kent in 1943, and made famous by Bing Crosby.
2   A phrase coined by the English translator of Dietrich Bonhoeffer's classic, *The Cost of Discipleship* (1937).
3   A phrase attributed to St Francis of Assisi (1181–1226).
4   A line from the hymn 'Great is thy faithfulness', written by Thomas Chisholm in 1923.
5   Brother Lawrence (c.1614–91) was a lay brother in a Carmelite monastery. His small classic *The Practice of the Presence of God* has gone through many editions and is currently available from Wilder Publications (2008) as well as various other publishers.
6   Marie Phillips, *Gods Behaving Badly* (Vintage, 2008).
7   Tom Wright, *Luke for Everyone* (SPCK, 2001), p. 127.
8   A line from the hymn 'Through all the changing scenes of life' (Nahum Tate and Nicholas Brady, 1698).
9   *Groundhog Day* was directed by Harold Ramis and issued in 1993. It's based on the premise of a man who is consigned to repeating the same day over and over again.
10   Gordon Wenham, *Numbers* (IVP, 1981), p.164.
11   See note 1 above.
12   The first line of the chorus of a song written by Johnson Oatman Jr. in 1897.
13   C.S. Lewis, 'The weight of glory', first preached in the church of St Mary the Virgin, Oxford, on 8 June 1942, and most recently published in *The Weight of Glory and Other Addresses* (Zondervan, 2001).
14   A line from the hymn 'God of grace and God of glory', written by Harry Fosdick in 1930.
15   Oliver James, *Affluenza* (Vermilion, 2007).
16   'Lest we forget' is a line from Kipling's 1897 poem 'Recessional', which is often added to the end of the 'Ode to Remembrance', itself an extract of a poem by Lawrence Binyon.
17   A line from the famous Kipling poem 'If' (first published in 1910).
18   Richard Foster, *Money, Sex and Power* (Hodder and Stoughton, 1999).

19 Mel Gibson's *The Passion of the Christ* was first released in 2004. It includes scenes of graphic brutality and its dialogue is entirely conducted in a reconstructed Aramaic, Latin and Hebrew.

20 A line from the hymn 'Praise, my soul, the king of heaven, a metrical version of Psalm 103 written by Henry F. Lyte in 1834.

21 A verse from the famous Good Friday hymn 'When I survey the wondrous cross' (Isaac Watts, 1707).

22 Tom Wright, *John for Everyone Part 2* (SPCK, 2002), p. 146.

Also by Andrew Watson

THE FOURFOLD LEADERSHIP
OF JESUS

Come, follow, wait, go

'Don't follow me. Follow Jesus!' runs a popular slogan. The apostle Paul wrote, 'Follow my example, as I follow the example of Christ.' Can we ever hope to echo Paul's words—or should we only point away from ourselves to Jesus?

This book explores what it means to lead as Jesus led. He called his disciples to come, to follow, to wait and to go—commands that embody four different aspects of leadership, which can be a model for us today. As we follow Jesus, we are transformed into his likeness by the Holy Spirit. Disciples become leaders, who in turn nurture more disciples, so that the work of God's kingdom continues to grow, and we can dare to echo Paul's bold words.

ISBN 978 1 84101 435 7   £7.99
Available to order at the website www.brfonline.org.uk, or from your local Christian bookshop.

Also by Andrew Watson

CONFIDENCE IN THE LIVING GOD

David and Goliath revisited

As Christians, we are called to proclaim our faith in God, but how can we build and maintain this confidence in an increasingly secularised culture where such faith is often seen as marginal, embarrassing or even downright dangerous?

Using the story of David and Goliath, Andrew Watson takes a narrative theology approach to show how the Lord can indeed be our confidence, whatever the odds. He explores how God can develop a proper self-confidence within individuals and his Church, revealing the gospel through transforming words and transformed lives. he considers, too, how we can confidently tackle the challenges of day-to-day living, whether a difficult work situation or family relationship, or simply anxiety about the future. The book includes a study guide and is ideal as a whole church course on the subject of confidence.

ISBN 978 1 84101 643 6   £7.99
Available to order at the website www.brfonline.org.uk, or from your local Christian bookshop.

Also from BRF

MEET JESUS

A call to adventure

John Twisleton

To engage with Jesus expands the mind and heart. It challenges our view of the way the world is, where it is heading and what difference we could make to it. But in a world of competing philosophies, where does Jesus fit in? How far can we trust the Bible and the Church? What difference does Jesus make to our lives and our communities? Is Jesus really the be all and end all?

Meet Jesus is a lively and straightforward exploration of these and other questions, with the aim of engaging our reason, inspiring our faith and worship, deepening our fellowship and service, and bringing new depth to our witness to the world. Each chapter ends with some practical points for action and the book concludes with a section of discussion material for groups.

ISBN 978 1 84101 895 9   £7.99
Available to order at the website www.brfonline.org.uk, or from your local Christian bookshop.

Also from BRF

WHOLE LIFE, WHOLE BIBLE

50 readings on living in the light of Scripture

Antony Billington
with Margaret Killingray and Helen Parry

Where we spend most of our time—at home, at work, in the neighbourhood—matters to God and to his mission in and for the world. Far from restricting our faith to the 'personal' sphere, disengaged from everyday living, scripture encourages us to take the Lord of life into the whole of life.

Whole Life, Whole Bible is written from the conviction that God's word illuminates every part of existence, enabling us to see differently and live differently—from Monday to Sunday, in public as well as in private. A walk through the unfolding story of the Bible in 50 readings and reflections shows how our lives are bound up with, and shaped by, God's plan to restore a broken universe. That big story forms our minds, fuels our imaginations and fashions our daily life as we live in God's world, in the light of God's word, wherever we are.

ISBN 978 0 85746 017 2   £6.99   Available from January 2012
Available to order at the website www.brfonline.org.uk, or from your local Christian bookshop.

ENJOYED READING THIS LENT BOOK?

Did you know BRF publishes a new Lent and Advent book each year? All our Lent and Advent books are designed with a daily printed Bible reading, comment and reflection. Some can be used in groups and contain questions which can be used in a study or reading group.

Previous Lent books have included:

Jesus Christ—the Alpha & the Omega, Nigel G. Wright
Giving It Up, Maggi Dawn
Fasting and Feasting, Gordon Giles
Journey to Jerusalem, David Winter

> If you would like to be kept in touch with information about our forthcoming Lent or Advent books, please complete the coupon below.

❏ Please keep me in touch by post with forthcoming Lent or Advent books
❏ Please email me with details about forthcoming Lent or Advent books

Email address: _____

Name _____

Address_____

_____

_____

Postcode _____

Telephone_____

Signature _____

Please send this completed form to:

Freepost RRLH-JCYA-SZX
BRF, 15 The Chambers,
Vineyard, Abingdon,
OX14 3FE, United Kingdom

Tel. 01865 319700
Fax. 01865 319701
Email: enquiries@brf.org.uk

www.brf.org.uk

PROMO REF: END/LENT12

For more information, visit the **brf** website at **www.brf.org.uk**

Enjoyed this book?

Write a review—we'd love to hear what you think.
Email: reviews@brf.org.uk

Keep up to date—receive details of our new books as they happen.
Sign up for email news and select your interest groups at:
www.brfonline.org.uk/findoutmore/

Follow us on Twitter @brfonline

By post—to receive new title information by post (UK only), complete the form below and post to: BRF Mailing Lists, 15 The Chambers, Vineyard, Abingdon, Oxfordshire, OX14 3FE

Your Details
Name _____
Address_____
_____
Town/City _____ Post Code _____
Email_____

Your Interest Groups (*Please tick as appropriate)

- ☐ Advent/Lent
- ☐ Bible Reading & Study
- ☐ Children's Books
- ☐ Discipleship
- ☐ Leadership

- ☐ Messy Church
- ☐ Pastoral
- ☐ Prayer & Spirituality
- ☐ Resources for Children's Church
- ☐ Resources for Schools

Support your local bookshop
Ask about their new title information schemes.